ACADEMY OF
LEARNING

Your Complete Preschool Lesson Plan Resource: Volume 8

© 2015 Breely, Crush & Associates, LLC

Ver. 112214

Table of Contents

Educator Biography

Sharlit Elliott has a B.S. in Elementary Education and Early Childhood from Brigham Young University and has been a teacher for over 15 years working with children ages 3-5. She keeps current on changes in education by attending University classes and conferences several times a year. Besides having raised five children, she has held various leadership positions with the Girl Scouts and the 4-H program. She enjoys gardening, scrapbooking, reading and of course working with children.

How to Use This Book

This book is designed for a teacher working with children ages 3-5 in a classroom, homeschool or home preschool environment. One of the most important aspects of this series is that it includes fun activities that will enhance their skills. These lessons plans, games and ideas are all for you to use. Don't forget, these are complete lessons and activities that have been designed for compliance with federal and state guidelines for education. We go above and beyond to bring you MORE than what's expected in the public school system.

We will refer to your students as "your children or class". That includes whatever area you are using these lessons for: homeschool or preschool. Our lesson plans include improving student's abilities through activities. The skills we will be working with include: listening skills, music, movement, language and literacy, mathematics, science, fine motor, creative art, sensory, dramatic play, and social skills.

The book is organized by themes which will help you quickly find just the right information. The headings in the book will direct you quickly to large group, small group, and free time activities. It will also provide ideas for field trips.

This book will include the following areas:

Group Activities/Circle Time

- Music & Movement is used to help develop large muscles in arms and legs. These need to be developed before children can be successful in small muscles activities such as used in writing or cutting with scissors. This area also helps children learn to enjoy music and the basics such as beat, loud/soft and fast/slow.

- Language & Literacy is how we help children learn vocabulary, story order, thinking skills, recall, concepts of the theme, and expressive language.

Small Group Activities/Table Times

- Math & Cognitive is used to teach numbers, shapes, patterns, sorting, thinking and reasoning skills.

- Fine Motor Skills develop small muscles to be able to draw, write, manipulate small things, to tear, and to cut with scissors.

- Language & Literacy is used to develop skills such as expressive writing, visual memory, matching letters, letter sounds, categorizing items, directional words, and opposites.

- Other creative activities to develop their own uniqueness as an individual.

Free Time

- Creative arts to draw, build, and develop their imagination.

- Sensory activities are used to learn through exploration and using their senses.

- Dramatic Play & Social Development let children take on different roles, solve problems, find solutions, and develop social interactions.

- Science helps children explore by experimenting, identifying problems, guessing what will happen, checking to see what did happen, questioning how things happened, and developing a plan of what to do next.

- Gross Motor Skills to practice using large and small muscles in fun activities.

- Field Trip Ideas to help children use real places to learn about the world.

Throughout the book we will use the following icons to show the different types of activities:

MUSIC & MOVEMENT

LANGUAGE & LITERACY

MATH & COGNITIVE

FINE MOTOR SKILLS

CREATIVE ARTS

SENSORY

DRAMATIC PLAY & SOCIAL DEVELOPMENT

SCIENCE

GROSS MOTOR SKILLS

FIELD TRIP IDEAS

Spring & Weather

GROUP ACTIVITIES/CIRCLE TIME

MUSIC AND MOVEMENT

"Over in the Meadow" from "Dr. Jean Sings Silly Songs" by Dr. Jean.

"Bringing Home A Baby Bumble Bee" from "Dr. Jean Sings Silly Songs" by Dr. Jean.

"The Butterfly" from "Dr. Jean Sings Silly Songs" by Dr. Jean. The songs cited here are fun songs for the children and you can do actions to the words in the songs.

"Tooty Ta" from "Dr. Jean & Friends" by Jean Feildman. This song has everyone laughing as you follow the actions that the words tell you to do.

"Weather Song" from "Dr. Jean & Friends" by Jean Feildman. This song sings about the different types of weather that children can act out and it provides the sounds of the different types of weather.

"The Water Cycle" from "Kiss Your Brain!" by Dr. Jean. This song teaches children to use arm movements to teach the cycle of water.

"Seasons" from "Kiss Your Brain!" by Dr. Jean. This song talks about the different elements of the four seasons.

"Weather Song" from "Ole! Ole! Ole!" by Dr. Jean. This is such a great song to sing everyday because children sing about the type of weather that they are having that day. There are verses for sunny, cloudy, rainy, and snowy. You can play the song in English and in Spanish. This CD also has many other songs in English and Spanish.

"A Conversation With a Tree" from "Touched by a Song" by Miss Jackie. www.jackiesilberg.com. This song teaches children that we get shade, fruit, nuts and beauty from trees.

"Spring Flowers," "Slow Day" and "Sunflower" songs are from "Quiet Time" by Raffi. These songs are great for bring some calm in to your day. www.raffines.com.

"The Garden Song," "Each of Us is a Flower" and "May There Always Be Sunshine" are from "10 Carrot Diamond" by Charlotte Diamond. These songs are great movement songs with a lively tempo.

"In the Woods There Was a Tree" and "What a Wonderful World!" are from Just For Fun! by Dr. Jean. These songs help them become aware of the world around them and have fun while learning.

LANGUAGE AND LITERACY

Introduce this unit by asking the children what they know about spring and weather. Use a wipe off board or a chalk board to write the theme words in the center. Then draw lines out from the circle as children tell you things they know about. Record what the children say at the end of the lines going out from the center. In this way you can better understand what books and activities reflect their interests and build on the knowledge that they already have.

This is also a good time to have children become more aware of the weather. Talk about how the sky looks each day and if it's windy, sunny, cloudy, rainy, snowy or any combination of these things. It's fun to sing songs about the weather and have the children draw their own pictures to represent the different types of weather. Then you can use their pictures at the circle when talking or singing about the weather. Also have them watch for and tell you about what's happening with the trees, shrubs and plants that they see outside.

A Letter To Amy by Ezra Jack Keats, Harper & Row, Publishers.

Watching The Seasons by Edana Eckart, Scholastic Inc.

Weather A First Discovery Book, Scholastic Inc.

Clifford's Spring Clean-Up by Norman Bridwell, Scholastic Inc. Children really love Clifford books. This book points out in a fun way what people often do in the spring.

The Year At Maple Hill Farm by Alice and Martin Provensen, A Jonathan Cape Book.

Cloudy With a Chance of Meatballs by Judi Barrett, Scholastic Inc. This is a fun book and great for children imaginations.

Wind by Susan Canizares – Betsey Chessen, Scholastic Inc. This book has great photographs of the wind.

Water by Susan Canizares - Pamela Chanko, Scholastic Inc.

Storms by Susan Canizares – Betsey Chessen, Scholastic Inc.

Splish, Splash, Spring by Jan Carr, Scholastic Inc.

A Book of Seasons by Alice and Martin Provensen, A Random House Pictureback.

Weather by Pamela Chanko – Daniel Moreton, Scholastic Inc.

It Looked Like Spilt Milk by Charles G. Shaw, Scholastic Inc. This is a fun book that will inspire children to look at cloudy and see their many shapes.

Watching the Weather by Edana Eckart Scholastic Inc.

Watching the Wind by Edana Eckart, Scholastic Inc.

Amy Loves the Rain by Julia Hoban, Harper Collins Publishers.

Amy Loves the Wind by Julia Hoban, Scholastic Inc.

Amy Loves the Sun by Julia Hoban, Scholastic Inc.

Water's Way by Lisa Westberg Peters, Scholastic Inc. This story is about how water changes and moves to form cloudy and returns to earth in many ways, such as rain and snow.

The Little House by Virginia Lee Burton, Scholastic Inc. This book is a Caldecott Book.

Rain by Marion Dane Bauer, Scholastic Inc. This book tells about all the wonders of rain.

Clouds by Marion Dane Bauer, Scholastic Inc. This books tells about all the wonders of clouds.

My Favorite Time of Year by Susan Pearson, Scholastic Inc.

Rain Drops Splash by Alvin Tresselt, Scholastic Inc.

Whatever the Weather by Karen Wallace, DK Publishing, Inc.

Outside, Inside by Carolyn Crimi, Scholastic Inc.

Days, Months and Seasons Work Book, Peter Pan Industries.

When Spring Comes by Robert Maass, Scholastic Inc. Great photographs of people doing things in the spring.

Hopper Hunts for Spring by Marcus Pfister, Scholastic Inc.

Little Cloud by Eric Carle, Scholastic Inc. A simplified story of how rain comes.

Franklin And The Thunderstorm by Paulette Bourgeois – Brenda Clark, Scholastic Inc. Franklin's friends help him be safe and not frightened of the storm.

Mud by Mary Lyn Ray, Scholastic Inc.

Puddles by Jonathan London, Scholastic Inc. This is a fun book about after the rain stops and puddle jumping begins.

The Wind Blew by Pat Hutchins, Scholastic Inc.

The Rainy Day Alphabet Book by Jackie Posner and Sara Wiener, Scholastic Inc.

Clifford The Big Red Dog: The Storm Day Rescue by Norman Birdwell, Scholastic Inc.

A Nest Full of Eggs by Priscilla Belz Jenkins, Scholastic Inc.

SMALL GROUP ACTIVITIES/TABLE TIMES

MATH & COGNITIVE

Umbrella Handle Match

Prepare several sets of umbrella tops with numerals 1-10 on them. Use colorful construction paper for the tops. See simple patterns. Then make simple cane shaped handles for them. Do not use matching colors for the handle with the top, if you do it will become a matching color game instead of a learning number activity. Place dots on the handles representing the numerals 1-10. Laminate them and place each set in an individual bag.

Now have a few of the children come to the table. Explain to the children that they are going to match the dots on the handles with the correct numeral of the umbrella top. Give them each a bag and tell them to begin. Walk around and help children where needed.

Spring Shape Match

Draw four clouds on white construction paper and make enough clouds for each child in the small group to have a set of nine clouds. Now draw eighteen rain drops on a piece of white card stock. Make enough copies for each child in your small group to have a set of nine raindrops. Then draw each of these shapes on a rain drop to make a set: triangle, circle, diamond, rectangle, star, heart, square, oval and a crescent. Make the same drawings on each of the nine clouds, so they can match the cloud shape and the raindrop shape together. Children will be working with a partner at the table so they will be sharing one set per two children. See example.

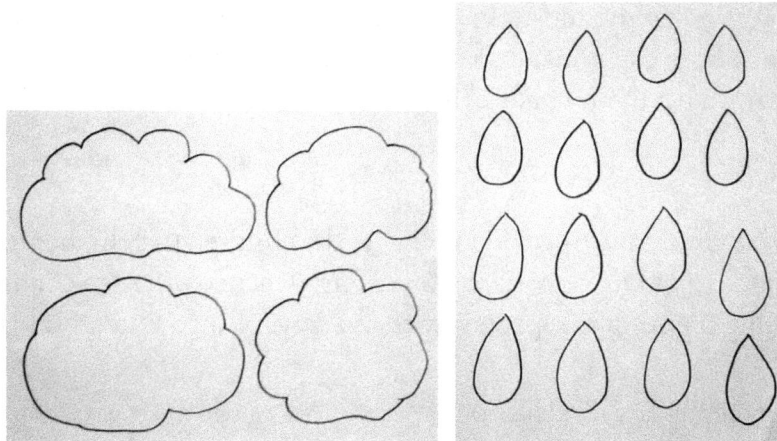

Now cut out the individual clouds and rain drops to make sets and laminate them. Place each set in a bag. When children come to the table, have them choose or you choose a partner for them. Tell children that in this game they will work as partners. One child will match the shape of the rain drop to the cloud that has the same shape on it. Then the other child will tell the name of the shape on it. Then the first child will make a match again with a different shape and the second child will name it. They will continue in this manner until all of the nine clouds have been matched to a rain drop.

Now the children will take off all the matches and start over again, but the first child will be the one to name the shapes and the second child will match the shapes. Play will continue until all nine of the shapes have been matched and named.

Butterfly Fun

For this activity the teacher will buy bags of bow tie noodles. Then turn them into butterflies by coloring the noodles. You can do this by placing noodles into a zip lock bags with several drops of food coloring and a small amount of rubbing alcohol. Next zip the bag closed and shake it. You can also do this using liquid water colors from a school supply store. Then you don't need to use the rubbing alcohol, making it safer. Liquid water colors will also make much brighter colored butterflies.

After shaking them in the bag, place them onto several layers of paper towels to dry. Make sure that the noodles are dry before they are used by the children. Make at least four different colors. When all the noodles are dried, mix the noodles up and place a handful of the colorful butterflies into zip lock bags. You will need to have one for each of the children that will come to the table at one time. Then the same bags of noodles can be used by the next group of children.

Now have the children come to the table and give each child a bag of the pretend butterflies. Ask them to sort the noodles by color. Next have them and count each color and see which group has the most. To extend this activity to another day, use the same noodles again, but have them make a two color pattern with the noodles. If they can do a two color pattern have them make a three color pattern and then a four color pattern.

Ten Frogs

Sing the song "Five Green and Speckled Frogs" to the children to help them get acquainted with it. This song is an old nursery rhyme and song. Teacher will then change the number of frogs to ten. Sing the song except start with ten frogs and go until you reach zero frogs.

Five green and speckled frogs,

Sat on a speckled log,

Eating some most delicious bugs,

Yum, Yum.

One jumped into the pool,

Where it was nice and cool,

Now there are four green speckled frogs,

Glub, glub.

Four green and speckled frogs,

Sat on a speckled log,

Eating some most delicious bugs,

Yum, yum.

One jumped into the pool,

where it was nice and cool,

Now there are three green speckled frogs,

Glub, glub.

Three green and speckled frogs,

Sat on a speckled log,

Eating some most delicious bugs,

Yum, Yum.

One jumped into the pool,

Where it was nice and cool,

Now there are two green speckled frogs,

Glub, glub.

Two green and speckled frogs.

Sat on a speckled log,

Eating some most delicious bugs,

Yum, Yum.

One jumped into the pool,

Where it was nice and cool,

Now there is one green speckled frog,

Glub, glub.

One green and speckled frog,

Sat on a speckled log,

Eating some most delicious bugs,

Yum, yum.

He jumped into the pool,

Where it was nice and cool,

Now there are no green speckled frogs,

Glub, glub.

For this activity the teacher will draw or copy a pictures of frogs. You will need to make 10 of them. Also use a large piece of blue paper to create a pond. Write a numbers from 1-10 on each frog.

14

To play this game, give out two frogs to five children, making sure that the numbers given out are not in order. Have the children put their frogs on the table in front of them and have them count all the frogs. Then have the children sing the song with you by start with ten frogs. When you sing "one jumped in the pool," have the child with the frog (numbered 10) put it into the pool.

Continue singing the song and when you come to the part of the song "now there are nine green speckled frogs" have the children count with you how many frogs are left on the table - nine. Then continue the song. Now sing as before, "Nine green and speckled frogs, sat on a speckled frog, Eating some most delicious bugs, Yum, Yum." Then do as before have the child with the number nine frog put it into the pond when singing, "one jumped into the pool where it was nice and cool" and continue as before until you have all the frogs in the pond and have sung all the verses. This activity will help learning to count to ten, what look different numeral look like and help them to recognize the amount each number represents. See example.

Flower Bingo

Make bingo cards by creating a simple pattern of a spring flower on card stock. Draw two leaves with a stem coming up the middle of it. Then make five petals on the stem with a circle in the middle for the center. Now add dots to represent numbers 1- 6 by making each number on a petal and one on the center. Then make additional cards in the same manner. Making each card with the dots on the petals in a different order on the card.

Teacher will now make petal markers by making petals using colored construction paper that fit the petals drawn on the cards. Each petal will have a numeral written on it from 1-6. Also make a circle marker for the center of the flower with a number on it. You will need to make one set for each of the bingo cards you made for your small group. You can color in the leaves and stem on the cards or cut green construction paper and glue over the stem and leaves on the bingo cards. See example.

For this game the children will take turns shaking a die and adding a petal or center to their bingo card. They place the correct number where that many dots appear on their card. For example, three dots on a petal with numeral three written on it. If they already have it they may shake the die one additional time to make a match before their turn is over. Then the next player takes the die and shakes and places a matching number over the correct number of dots. Play continues until each child has their card has all the dots covered with the correct numerals. When one card has been filled, the child says bingo and that child can go to another table.

Cloud Fun

You will need to make a pattern for this activity. Turn a paper sideways so that the long side is in front of you and draw three lines across the 11 1/2 inch page about 2 inches apart. Then draw a column four inches from the left hand side from the top to the bottom. Now draw a numeral one in the first row with a cloud next to it and a dot representing the numeral one.

Now go to the next row and choose a numeral you want them to learn or use the numeral two to make it easier and draw a cloud with two dots inside it. Then write another numeral or use the numeral three and draw another cloud with three dots in it.

Then go to the third row and continue by choose a numeral and put that amount of dots in a cloud. Do the same thing with the forth row. Make copies of this sheet, so that you have one for each of the children and one to keep as a master for yourself. Buy a bag of cotton balls and have enough small bottles of glue for children to use at the table.

Children will say the numeral name and count the dots in the cloud next to it. Then they will take that many cotton balls and put balls out to make them look like fluffy clouds and glue in the row across the correct number of clouds that match the numeral. Then they will continue to the next rows and do the same thing. See example of sheet.

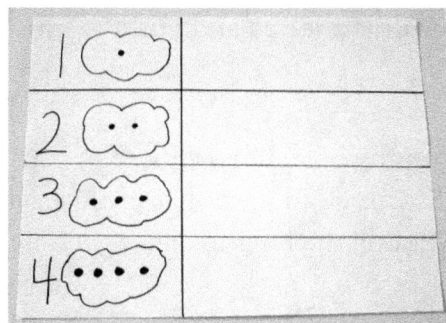

Easter Egg Counting

Use saved empty egg cartons for this activity. Also buy plastic Easter eggs around Easter to get them inexpensively. You will need a dozen eggs and one egg carton for each child in your small group. Use a permanent marker to write a numeral from 1-12 on each egg top. Then use the marker to make that number of dots on the bottom to match the numeral on the top. Provide colorful cereal such as frost O's or fruit loops and place a handful of cereal in a snack size plastic bag for each child to use. Fill each carton with the number 1-12 marked eggs.

Have the children come to the table and give them each a carton of eggs and a sack of cereal. Tell them to take out a plastic egg. Now they will put that many pieces of cereal into it as the number written on the plastic eggs indicates. Or if they can't tell what number it is they should count the dots on the egg to learn how many pieces to put into the egg. After they have filled the egg have them close it and put it back into the carton and pick up another egg. They should keep filling the eggs until all of them have been filled.

Then have them say each number on the egg to you. Help them put the eggs back into the carton in correct order. Now they can eat the cereal in the eggs after dumping them into their snack bag.

FINE MOTOR SKILLS

Storm Cutting

Make a large cloud on poster board. Then trace around it on gray construction paper for children to use scissor skills to cut on the lines and make a cloud. Another idea to use would be to have the children trace around the cloud pattern themselves and cut it out. See example.

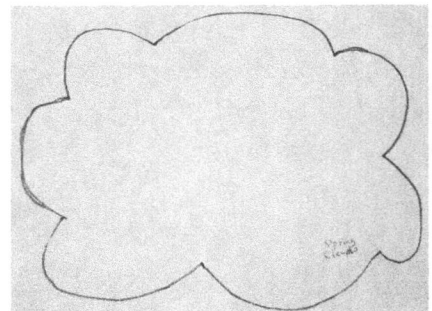

Teacher will make a large lightning bolt across a piece of construction paper and transfer the pattern to poster board. The children will use this pattern on a piece of yellow construction paper and then cut on the lines to create their lightning bolt to go with their cloud. See example.

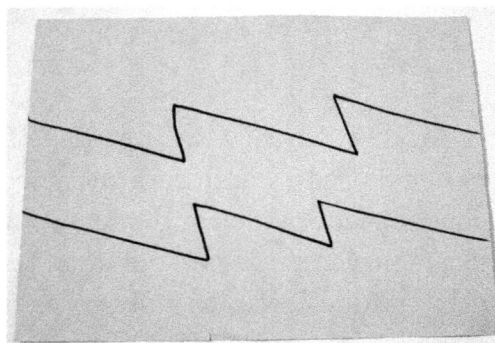

Hand Print Flowers

Prepare leaves and stems by drawing a pattern and tracing it onto green construction paper. Then children can cut out a pattern and the teacher can have additional ones cut out for them to use. Prepare the additional ones by placing the pattern on construction paper as many times as you can fit it on one sheet. Then place it on top of four sheet of green construction paper and staple around the edges so the paper will not move as you cut through all five sheets at one time. Repeat this process until you have an adequate supply of extra ones. See example.

The teacher will mix poster paint with dish detergent in several spring colors and place the paint onto a plastic dinner plates. Place aprons or paint shirts out for the children to keep their clothes clean. Tell children they will be making spring flowers and that everyone will need to cut out one stem for this activity and glue it onto a piece of paper. They can glue the green plant part onto their paper and they may also glue two extra ones from the table if they would like a couple more.

Now they put on paint aprons and place their whole hand into the spring color of paint and them press their hand on to the paper with the bottom of their hand on the stem. Their fingers can be spread out or tight together to make their flower. Make a flower on the next stem if they have another one glued on and continue until each stem has a flower hand print. Have them go to the sink after this and wash their hands first into a pail of warm soapy water and then at the sink and dry them. Make sure that each paper has the child's name on it. Hang them up in your room when they are dry or let them take them home.

Spring Scene

For this activity have colored construction paper available, small glue bottles, white and yellow cotton balls, small googly eyes, markers, small colored feathers, scissors and plastic grass (find grass at Easter time).

Children will use the materials to make a spring picture on pieces of construction paper. They may glue across bottom of picture and apply the plastic grass. They may also use white cotton balls to make clouds by pulling them and then gluing them in the sky.

They can also use cotton balls to make bunnies. The bunny ears can be made by children cutting small ear shape pieces from white paper and gluing them on top of the cotton ball. Then they could glue on the googly eyes.

Ducks or chickens can be made using yellow or white cotton balls and the small googly eyes. Children can cut beaks or bills using orange construction paper and then glue them to the top of their cotton balls. Children can also use the small feathers for ducks or chickens. They can use the markers to draw themselves, trees, hills, sky, flowers and etc.

Wind Socks

Use large double wide construction paper in bright colors for this project. Fold the paper in half. By doing this it will look like one regular piece of construction paper. Draw a line across the top of the paper that is 3 inches wide. Next make 3 columns from the line across to the bottom making them a little less than 3 inches wide. Then open the folded section and extend the top line across of this sheet. See example.

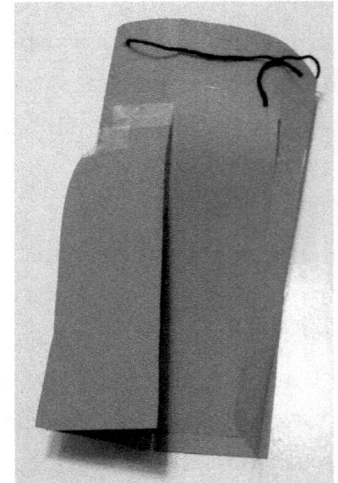

Children will keep paper folded while cutting from the bottom up to the line across the top on the two column lines. Then they will open up the folded section and cut on the folded line from the bottom up to the line across the top. Now loop the ends together and staple at the top to form the wind sock. They can now use a hole punch to make a hole at the top on each side, so that they can hang it to blow in the wind. Provide them with a piece of yarn that is about 28 inches long. They will thread the yarn through the holes and tie the ends together.

Then provide stickers for them to decorate their wind sock and have them write their name so they will know which one is theirs.

Spring Rainbow

Prepare a sheet of paper to copy for the children to do this project. Draw six lines with about a little over ½ spacing between them to form a rainbow in the sky. Under the rainbow write "Spring brings rainbows." Make enough copies of this page for each child in the class, but work on the sheet in small groups.

Now use a paper cutter to make cuts across sheets of colored construction paper in the colors of the rainbow: violet, blue, green, yellow, and red. You will need one strip of color for each child in the class.

When children come to the table explain that they will be making a rainbow. Have a book that shows a rainbow, so that the children will know how one looks. Point out that the colors are the same on each row and not mixed on a row. Provide small bottles of glue for the children to use. Tell them they will need to tear one strip of a color at a time.

Then they will glue the color pieces in one row between the lines. When the rainbow pictures are dry, hang them around the classroom. Tearing is good way to develop their fine motor skills. See example.

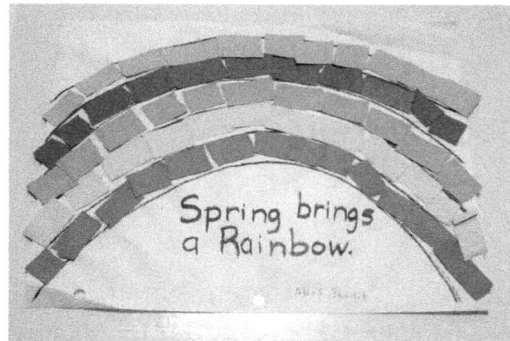

Umbrella Fun

Draw a large umbrella shape and place it on four other pieces of colored construction paper. Then staple around the pattern and cut through all the pages at one time. Use this same pattern on the next stack of construction paper and staple and cut it as before. Continue in this manner until you have enough tops for your class and one for your file.

Now make a large handle shape for the umbrella. Place it on top of four pieces of construction paper and staple it. Then cut it as you did with the tops. Now use the paper cutter to cut small squares from bright colors of tissue paper or crepe paper. Other items for children to use could be small strands of silver plastic found as a craft store could represent rain. Sequins could also be used and anything else like colored bow noodles would be fun to use.

Children will come to the table and choose a colored umbrella top and a colored handle. Then glue the handle on to their umbrella. Then they will choose from the different materials and glue them on to their umbrella. These bright umbrellas will brighten up your classroom even of cloudy days. See example.

Glitter Kites

Create a simple kite pattern for the children to trace onto colored construction paper. Children will cut their kite. Provide small bottles of glue for the children. They will use the glue to draw designs on their kite. Then give them shaker bottles with glitter in them, which children will use to shake onto the wet glue.

When they have covered their glue with glitter have them carefully lift their kites and let excess glitter fall off onto a tray. You can use the excess glitter another day by saving it and pouring it back into a glitter bottle. Let the kites dry well before sending them home.

LANGUAGE AND LITERACY

Kite Tail Patterning

Provide a simple kite pattern for children as in "glitter kites." They can trace and cut as in the "glitter kites." Or you can cut the kites out by placing a pattern on top of four pieces of construction paper, stapling around edges and cutting them out as in before procedures mentioned in "umbrella fun."

Supply colored squares of crepe paper in two or three different colors, small bottles of glue or tape and pieces of yarn for each of the kites.

Next, hide around the classroom items that have patterns for the children to find. These items could be a checker board, plaid material, beads strung on a pipe cleaner, boarders around the bulletin board, or items patterned in a egg carton.

Now children will come to the table and teacher will show and explain what a simple pattern looks like. Then using two colors of crepe paper, teacher will make a pattern using squares of the colored crepe paper. Children will next go looking as a small group for patterns in the classroom. If they need help, give them clues so they can find the items you have hidden. Ask the children if they can see patterns on their clothing. Make sure you wear something with a pattern today for them to discover.

After finding patterns, have them make a tail for a kite. They will use the yarn and glue on the colored squares. If they are having trouble gluing the squares onto the tail let them use tape. Tell them they can make a two color pattern and if they want to try a three color pattern they can. Help them if needed.

It Looked Like Spilt Milk

After reading the book <u>Sometimes It Looks Like Spilt Milk</u>, have the each child create their own page for a classroom book. They will draw an item, like a pizza or something else that a cloud could look like. Since the items are really clouds, have the children draw on blue construction paper using white chalk. Then use the text from the book and write on the bottom of their picture, "Sometimes it looks like (name of drawing goes here), but it isn't." Do this at the bottom of each of their pictures. Then on the last page teacher will draw a big white cloud and write, "It is a big, white cloud in the blue sky!"

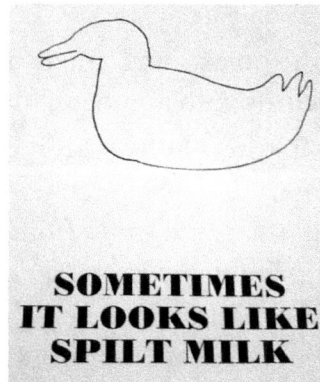

It looked like spilt milk, but it wasn't.

SOMETIMES IT LOOKS LIKE SPILT MILK

Next teacher will put the pictures in a loose leaf journal and have the children help her read their book. Then children can take turns reading the book. Make sure their name is included on their special page. They really love to read books when they have had a part in being an author and an illustrator!

Egg Hatch

You will need to buy a large plastic egg for this activity. Then buy a small Easter chick that will fit into the egg. Prepare small squares on card stock of all the capital letters in the alphabet. Laminate the letter squares individually. Have tape available to tape the letter to the chick. To prepare this game use the capital letters of the children's names in the small group you are working with. Tape the letter of a child's first name to the chick and place it inside the egg.

To play the game, have the child whose letter name is in the egg open it and tell what the letter name is. If the child does not know the letter name have the children in the group help name it. If they can't help, tell the child the letter and the sound that it makes. Then have all the children say the letter name and make the letter sound together. Next place another letter in the egg attached to the chick that represents another child's name in your group. Have that child open the egg and say the letter and ask if the child can say the sound that the letter makes. If the child doesn't know, have other children help. Now have all the children say the letter and sound. Continue with the next child as before until all the children have had a turn.

An extension of this game to do when the children are able to do their own first letter name and sound would be to have them learn the other children's names and sounds. After that, use the rest of the letters in the alphabet to learn the letter names and sounds.

Front and Back

Assemble items that have a clear front and back such as the following: boy or man's shirt with buttons and pocket, man or boy's pants with a zipper, toy truck, rain boot, rain coat, a book, a doll, a toy cash register, boy or girl's cap with a bill and a toy bike.

Hold up one of the objects and ask a child which part is the front and which part is the back. Then take turns with another child and have them tell and show you which part is the front and the back. Continue until all of the children have had a turn.

Then ask one child to stand up in front of the group. Now ask another child to tell you which is the child's front and back. Then have that child stand in front of the other child. Now ask another child to join the two children standing up and have the new child in front of the two children in line. Continue having the children come up and stand in front of in back of a child.

Now have them all sit down and ask one child to stand and ask the next child to come up and line up behind the first child. Continue until all of the children are standing up behind one another. Then have them all sit down again and have another child be in front and all the children to come up and be one behind the other. Watch and help where needed some will still not understand and will get in front of instead of behind. Practice this again another day by going through all the steps again.

Picture Stories

For this project, use pictures from magazines on flowers and spring. If you are unable to find these you can take your own photos of spring and/or spring or print them from the internet. Have the children come to your small group and show them a picture and tell them that you are going to make up a story about the pictures. Then tell them a short story using the picture.

Next tell them they are going to take turns, with the children in their group telling a story about a picture. Now tell children to pick a picture from the ones you have collected. Give them a few minutes to pick their picture and think of something that they could say about it. Tell them that their story should be about as long as a commercial break that they might see on T.V. This gives them a better idea or how long to take than an amount of minutes.

Before children start taking turns remind them to listen to the other's tell their story and think of something that they like about the other children's story, because they are going to take turns tell each person a good thing about their story when each child is finished with his or her story.

This might be fun to record each child telling their story and then playing them back during the coming weeks. Also, keep the pictures to show while listening to the story. Put the child's name on the picture to show which one they used.

FREE TIME

CREATIVE ARTS

Water Color Projects

Draw large rain drops and tulips. Then cut them out and use for a pattern and to make additional ones. Leave them on the table with paint aprons, watercolors, paint brushes and small cups of water to rinse their brushes. See example.

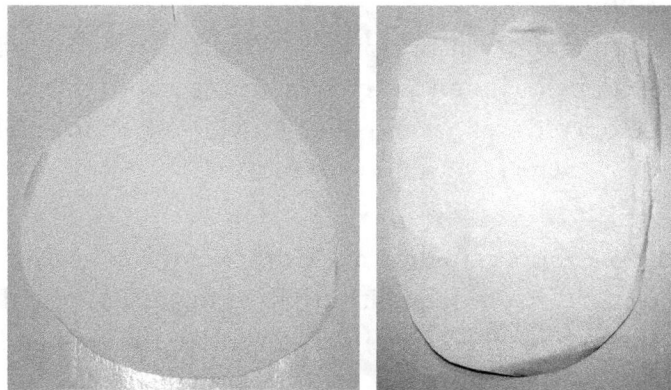

Pussy Willow and/or Forsythia

Place paper and brown crayons on the table. Children will draw sticks or branches going up at angles to represent the scrubs. Then if they want their picture to be pussy willows, have small bottles of glue and rice puff cereal in small bags for children to glue onto their branches.

If they want forsythia scrubs, provide small bottles of glue and small yellow pieces of crepe paper. They can glue them on the branches by putting a little glue down and yellow squares on them or by wrapping them around a pencil before touching them to the glue. See example.

SENSORY

Shaving Cream Rainbow

Use tubs or large trays for this sensory project. Teacher will prepare small cups with water and add a few drops of liquid watercolor to the cups. Use all the colors of the rainbow or primary colors red, yellow and blue. Provide eye droppers for children. Now shake and spray shaving cream onto trays and/ or tubs.

Children will use the eye droppers to drop a few drops of the colored water onto different areas of the shaving cream. They will mix it with their fingers to form the rainbow. When it's time to clean up they can well take their tray or tub to the sink and wash it off.

Rainbow Rice

Use liquid watercolors to color the rice for this activity. Put rice into a Ziploc bag and add liquid watercolor to bag. Start with a tablespoon of color, if you have a large amount of rice add a little more coloring. Mix until rice in bag is all colored the shade you want. You can add more coloring if you want it darker. Then spread it out onto newspapers to dry.

When it has dried thoroughly place it into a sensory table or tubs with funnels, scoops, clear plastic empty water bottles and other clear containers. Children love to measure, mix and pour the colored rice.

DRAMATIC PLAY & SOCIAL DEVELOPMENT

Camping

Set up an area of the classroom with camping props such as a small tent or a use a blanket over a card table if you do not have a tent. A small wading pool with paper laminate fish to catch in the pool. Place a paper clip on each fish. The poles will be dowels with a piece of yard tied onto one end of the pole and a strong magnet attached to the other end of the yarn. Camping dishes with pretend food goes well in this setting, along with small back packs and camp type clothing. Flashlights are lots of fun too. Make sure that you have extra batteries. Also it is fun to add stuffed animals such as bears, squirrels, birds and other animals you may find on a camping trip.

Other fun things might include an old Christmas tree or a large fake or real potted plant. Children could make their own birds or other animals out of paper to put in the tree. An inflatable raft would also be fun to use with a few a paddles, life jackets and fishing things. If you can find inexpensive toy binoculars buy a few pairs to use in your classroom for activities such as this. Dolls are also important for the family setting of the camp. If you have a small place for the dramatic play just use one large item like the tent or the raft with smaller items. It will still be fun for the children to pretend and develop their social skills.

Weather Station

Put up pictures of different types of clouds and weather, so that children can find matching types of clouds and weather. Have them look out the classroom window to make observations. Have paper attached to clip boards for children to draw the different types of weather that they see such as rain, snow, wind, clouds, and the sun. Put up a chart so they can tell for the different types of weather.

Have a thermometer in the classroom by the window and another one outside that they can see from the window. Help them learn to see areas on the thermometer that are hot and cold. Use a karaoke machine mike, so that have children can take turns giving the weather report at different times of the day. In the weather report have them tell the type of weather that they see and if it's hot, cold and in between. Also help them figure out what types of clothes to wear a that day.

Have different types of play clothes that they can wear over their clothing, to represent different types of clothing to wear when it is sunny, rainy, windy, snowy. Example would be warm coats, hats, mittens, boots, rain coats, umbrellas, sun hats, sunglasses and sweaters.

SCIENCE

Now is a good time to plant grass seed in a pot or two. Have children help you put the soil in and sprinkle the seeds. It works out best to have them use a small spray bottle to keep it watered. That way doesn't get over watered and it builds finger strength to spray it. Children enjoy watching it grow and when it gets tall, they can cut it carefully with scissors. It will keep growing like their lawn does.

You can also bring into the classroom a small branch or two of budding leaves of flowers. Place them in water so that the branch will last longer. Have the children observe it to see what happens.

Help children learn about wind by observing the wind blow a wind sock or a kite. Explain that the wind makes them move. We cannot see air or wind, but we can see it move things. Have children experiment with making air move by blowing from a straw onto a feather, a cotton ball, a ping pong ball, a pinwheel, and a plastic box. Ask them to think about the amount of air or blowing it took to move things. Did it take a lot of blowing to move light things and not much blowing?

Continue this discussion about the wind by going outside and flying a few kites. Let them feel the wind tugging on the string while the kite is flying. Or if there isn't enough wind to do that use this activity instead. You will need paper (freezer paper works best), but regular paper will do. Items also needed are diluted poster paint (use water to make it thin) and straws for each of the children.

Children will be blowing out through the straw, so have them practice before using with the paint. Tell them to place the straw between their lips and blow out onto their hand. Have them practice until they can feel the air coming out of the straw onto their hand. When they can do that place a small amount of the mixed paint on to their paper. Now have them blow through the straw at the paint. Have them watch the colored paint move across the paper. They can also use another color of paint and blow it too. This will make a new color if the two colors are blown together.

GROSS MOTOR SKILLS

Musical Egg

You will need a large Easter egg for this activity and small slips of paper. Write on the slips various actions that you want the children to do such as hop on their right/left foot, jump up and down, skip, gallop, touch their toes, do jumping jacks and run in place. Teacher can use the same egg for this activity by placing one of the slips into the egg after it has been read before passing it again.

Explain to the children that they will need to sit in circle and that she/he will play some music. They will pass the egg around to the person next to them in the circle until the music stops. Then the person who is holding the egg will open the egg. Teacher will read the slip and all the children will do the action that was on the slip. Then the teacher will place a new slip into the egg and play will resume again. Play will continue until all the slips have been used.

Another fun activity to get children moving is to play "Colored Easter Eggs." This old familiar game is played by choosing one child to be the wolf and the rest of the children to be the colored Easter eggs. Begin by having the children decide what color egg they will be. Teacher will also decide on the safe home place where the children will run to find safety.

Begin by having the wolf ask if there are any colored Easter eggs today. The eggs will answer yes and ask what color does he/she want. If the wolf guesses a color of an egg that one of the children picked, that child will run as fast as he/she can to the safe home. The wolf will try to tag the child. If the wolf does tag the egg before the child reaches home then that child becomes the wolf.

If the egg makes it home safe, the wolf goes back to the starting place and asks for another color of egg and chases that child. Play continues as before until wolf has gone through all the colors of the eggs or has caught a child. Then a new wolf is picked by the teacher and play continues until time allotted is over. Keep a list of the children that have been the wolf and next time you play choose someone who has not had a turn being the wolf.

FIELD TRIP IDEAS

Spring Walk

Make a card with small drawings of items that you want the children to locate on the walk such as – a flower in bloom, a leaf bud, a cloud in the sky, a worm on the ground, a flying insect, a crawling insect, a plant that is green, a small rock, a bird, the wind moving something and a small leaf. Make copies of the drawings for each child. In advance, take a walk around the area and decide where the best location for the walk will be.

Take a fanny pack with first aid items and a cell phone with important phone numbers with you on your walk with the children. Also take a camera with you and take photos of the children with the objects that they find. Invite any parents that would like to go with you to come and be sure and invite them ahead of time. Show the children the prepared paper of items to look for on the walk. Give them each a paper and a marker to cross off the items found on the walk.

Tell the children to look for the items on the page while the class goes for a short walk. When they see an item on the page they should say, "Look what I see." Then they should tell everyone what they see. Now that child can cross off that item. The other children can still look for that item as well as the other items. Continue on the walk until you have reached your predetermined place. Then go back the same way you came to give the children another opportunity to find the items found before or other spring items.

Extra Idea

Give each child a small sack to collect small items such as a leaf, small rock, small twigs or other small spring items. Be sure that they do not pick flowers from people's yards. If the area is a park or rural area, they may find wild flowers on weeds to pick, pine cones and other plants to put into their sack. When children get back to school, have them us the items they have collected to make a collage on a piece of construction paper. When they are dry place them around the room with the photos of the children find their items.

Plants – Fruits & Vegetables

GROUP ACTIVITIES/CIRCLE TIME

🎵 MUSIC AND MOVEMENT

"The Banana Song" from CD Jim Gill Sings The Sneezing Song and Other Contagious Tunes by Jim Gill.

"Mashed Potatoes" from CD Jim Gill Sings Do Re Mi On His Toe Leg Knee by Jim Gill.

"Fruit and Vegetable" from CD Touched by a Song by Miss Jackie.

"The Apple Seed" from CD Touched by a Song by Miss Jackie.

"The Mango Song" from CD Touched by a Song by Miss Jackie.

"Apples and Bananas" from CD Five Little Monkeys, Songs from Singing and Playing. This is a fun song that has children learning to make new words by changing the vowels in the words apple and banana.

"Parts Of A Flower" from CD Kiss Your Brain! by Dr. Jean. Children become the flower and do movements to act out the different parts of the flower.

"The Garden Song" from 10 CD Carrot Diamond by Charlotte Diamond from Hug Bug Records.

"Each of Us is a Flower" from CD Carrot Diamond by Charlotte Diamond from Hug Bug Records.

"Crunchy Carrots" from CD Carrot Diamond by Charlotte Diamond from Hug Bug Records.

"The Corner Grocery Store" from The Corner Grocery Store by Raffi. This is a fun song for children to act out using fingers to walk like knees, make circles with each thumb and index finger for glasses, thumbs twiddling, fingers playing horn and pretending to try on jeans. I made picture cards for the children for the song to help them know the words.

"The Farmer in the Dell" from Wee Sing presents Grandpa's Magical Toys by Price Stern Sloan. Just follow this old nursery song by joining hands, moving in a circle and picking different children to go inside the circle by naming them the farmer, then the wife, the child, the nurse, the dog, the cat, the rat and the last pick the cheese. Then it starts again by the rat picking the farmer. The farmer can be a girl and then she can pick the husband and so on.

"Pumpkins" from Macmillan Sing & Lean Program by Newbridge Communications, Inc.

"The Magic Seed" from Macmillan Sing & Lean Program by Newbridge Communications, Inc. Children use their bodies to act out this song. They start out being the tiny seed laying in a small ball on the floor and add wiggle toes for roots and continue on acting out the words in the song while growing into a blossoming plant.

"Growing Plants" from Macmillan Sing & Lean Program by Newbridge Communications, Inc. Children act out this song by being the gardener and working in different ways to help the seeds grow.

During this unit I usually add songs that are not always about the theme, but fun for them to sing such as the songs, "If You're Happy and You Know It" and "Simon Says from We All Live Together" Vol. 3 Greg Scelsa. Another one from that volume 3 is "Rock' Round The Mulberry Bush." When they have learned the song and actions change it using different words to the same tune. Example: This is the way to plants the seeds, plant the seeds, plant the seeds. This the way to plant the seeds so early in the morning. Make up other verses about the sun shining, rain watering, and harvesting the plant. Act out the song using different parts of their whole body, like wiggling fingers and moving them down to represent rain.

LANGUAGE AND LITERACY

The following books will help you bring out the different aspects of growing fruits and vegetables from planting them, caring for them and finally to harvesting them to eat and enjoy.

We Plant A Seed by Sharon Gordon, Troll Communications L.L.C.

One Bean by Anne Rockwell, Scholastic Inc.

All About Seeds by Melvin Berger, Scholastic Inc.

I'm A Seed by Jean Marzollo, Scholastic Inc.

From Seed To Plant by Gail Gibbons, Scholastic Inc.

A Seed Is A Promise by Claire Merrill, Scholastic Inc.

How A Seed Grows by Helene J. Jordan, Scholastic Inc.

Seeds Grow! by Angela Shelf Medearis, Scholastic Inc. This book includes game cards and other activities for Preschool – Grade 1.

What Shall I Grow? by Ray Gibson, Scholastic Inc. This is a great book with step by step instructions for great science growing projects.

The Garden In Our Yard by Greg Quinn, Scholastic Inc.

Round The Garden by Omri Glaser, Scholastic Inc.

Growing Vegetable Soup by Lois Ehlert, Scholastic Inc.

The Tale of Peter Rabbit by Beatrix Potter, Big Golden Book, Golden Press (Western Publishing Company, Inc.

Pumpkins Pumpkins by Jeanne Titherington, Scholastic Inc.

Mrs. McNosh and the Great Big Squash by Sarah Weeks, Scholastic Inc.

Jack and the Beanstalk Retold by Rita Balducci, A Golden Book Western Publishing Company, Inc.

Mickey and the Beanstalk by Walt Disney, Random House.

The Surprise Garden by Zoe Hall, Scholastic Inc.

It's Pumpkin Time! by Zoe Hall, Scholastic Inc.

The Carrot Seed by Ruth Krauss, Scholastic Inc.

The Enormous Carrot by Vladimir Vagin, Scholastic Inc.

The Little Mouse, The Red Ripe Strawberry, And The Big Hungry Bear by Don and Audrey Wood, Scholastic Inc.

The Apple Pie Tree by Zoe Hall, Scholastic Inc.

Who's Got The Apple? by Jan Loof, Random House PICTUREBACK.

Wide Wide World Supermarket Illustrated by George Fryer, Froebel-kan Co., Ltd.

Tops & Bottoms by Janet Stevens, Scholastic Inc. This is a fun book about how a bear got tricked out of his vegetables because he did not know the part of the plant that produced the different types of vegetables.

How Are You Peeling? by Saxton Freymann, Scholastic Inc. This book has beautiful pictures of vegetables and fruits with faces. You can tie this book into your unit and use it to talk about how we express our feelings. It was given an award of the Best Illustrated Children Book by the New York Times Book Review.

The Enormous Potato by Dusan Petricic, Scholastic Inc.

When reading books at the circle be sure and read the book yourself before reading it to the children. Relate the book to things that you are learning about and ask questions about things in the book to check for understanding as you go along through the book. Also, after reading the book ask for questions they have about the book. Let other children help with the answers where appropriate. Areas where there is a lot of interest need to be noted and bring in materials that goes along with the interests of the children. If a few of the children are more advanced and want to learn more, form a small group for them to learn more complex things without being boring to the other children.

SMALL GROUP ACTIVITIES/TABLE TIMES

MATH & COGNITIVE

Apple Matching Game

Make game cards for four or five children to use at one time by using shape of an apple. Place three apples on each card. Then add eyes, nose and mouth. Make each apple unique by having eyes both open, one eye open and one eye closed, both eyes closed. Then use different mouths such as smile, frown, surprised, silly. You can also have different shapes of noses and different colors of apples. After you have made four or five sets of unique apples, copy each unique set.

Glue three apples on each card and put the matching apples on a square to be placed over the matching apple. Continue this process until all the sets have been completed. Laminate them and place in a Ziploc bag. See example.

Children will each be given a long card with a set of small matching apple cards. They will need to look carefully to find the matching apples. You can have the children trade sets when they have completed their set correctly. This game uses thinking skills and careful observation by the children. You could also make this game using veggies or other fruits.

Count the Veggies

Use stickers of vegetables on squares for the children to sort into lines. When sorting is completed have the children count each line to see which line has the most and the least. You could also use fruit snack pieces to sort into lines and count or fruit loop cereal. Have them count to you and tell the most and least type of veggie, shape or color.

Homemade Potato Person Game

Buy a potato for each child in the class. Also assemble googly eyes for each, whole cloves for noses, paper shape for lips, short chenille pieces for arms, long pieces of chenille for legs and ribbon for belts. The belts can be tied around the middle of the potato. Children will use one die with dots 1-6 on it. Teacher will also need to make a chart for children to see with all the different body parts and the number required to obtain them on it. Example #1- body, #2- eye, #3- nose, #4- arm, #5- leg and #6- belt.

Tell the children that they will play the game by taking turns rolling the die. The number (1) must be rolled to start building the person, because the body is a one. You will only be able to have one body, so if you roll (1) again you will not get another body. The same rule applies for the number (3) which is the nose (a whole clove to be pushed into the potato) and the number (6) for a belt (a piece of ribbon tied on to the middle).

The number (2) will get you one eye and you must roll number (2) to get another eye. The number (4) is for one arm (short chenille) and must be rolled again to receive another one. The number (5) is for one leg (long chenille) and you must roll again for another one. The arms and legs are pushed into the potato.

To play this game children will take turns rolling the die, when they roll a (1) give them a potato. Each child must roll their own (1) to be given a body. Then they can roll any number that they need for more parts for their potato. The numbers do not have to be in order, but they are only allowed to get the correct number for each body part.

As the children roll the die have them count the dots and look at their chart to determine what body part they have earned. The child who gets all the body parts can go to the next activity if they want to or they can stay and watch the other children in their small group finish. Then you can call over a few more children to play and explain the game to them. Continue the game until everyone has had a turn.

You can save the game to be played another day by labeling them and placing them into the fridge. If you are not going to use them again send them home with each child.

Potatoes Growing in a Row

Label the top of a half sheet of paper "Five potatoes growing in a row." Make a line across the paper with rounded row lines for the potatoes. Then number the rows 1-5. Now cut out a set of five potatoes for each child with dots on each one from 1-5.

Children will each be given a page and a set of potatoes with a glue stick or bottle of glue. They will match the dot of the potato to the numeral of the row. When they have placed the potatoes in the rows have them check with you for correct order before they glue them on to the page. An example is shown.

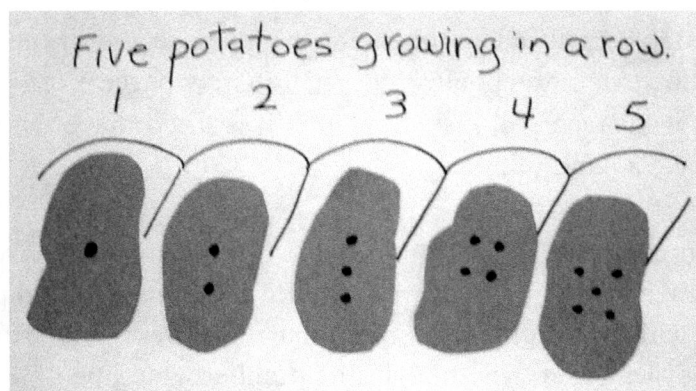

Name That Number

Use plant catalogs to find pictures of plants or create your own plants. Cut out pictures of plants and glue them on to a piece of paper. You will glue them in groups of 1-5, but do not glue groups in numeral order.

Then draw lines around each group and leave enough room to write number of plants. You will then draw dash lines that represent the number in each group.

Eventually, the children will count each group and then trace over the dash lines to make the number.

Make copies of this sheet for each of the children so that they can connect the amounts to the written numbers.

Another day after doing this page, have the children create their own number page by drawing their own objects in sections and have them write the correct number of the objects that they created. You could also copy their pages so that other children could do each other's pages. Then you could put them all into a number binder book that they could all look at and read. See example.

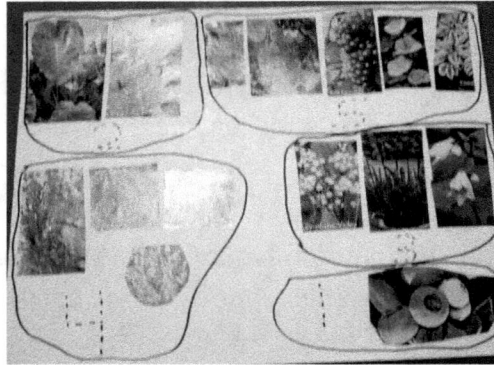

Sunflower

Plant and grow sunflowers ahead of time and save them to use in the classroom. After reading about sunflowers, in the book <u>What Shall I Grow</u> pages 4 & 5. Show your large sunflower head. If it is green still just show it. If it is dried, have the children in your small group each take a hand full of seeds.

Then have them guess (without counting them) how many they have and write that number down. Now have them take turns counting their seeds. Compare the number that they guessed with the number of seeds that there were. Ask if the number they guessed was more or less than they thought the number would be.

If you don't have time to plant and grow sun-flowers, use the drawings in the book or make some of your own and buy a package of sunflower seeds with the shell on them. They can take a small handful and guess how many they have like in the above example and still count and compare the numbers.

FINE MOTOR SKILLS

Fruit and Vegetable Prints

Supply fruits and vegetables that have been cut open to make prints, such as half of a green pepper, a large onion half, an ear of corn, an apple cut in the middle, a pear cut in half, a lemon cut in half and a orange. Prepare poster paint mixed with liquid dish soap in many colors and place some of each color of small foam plates.

Children will choose the fruits and vegetables to use as well and the paint color to dip them. Then they will dip them in color to print them on a large pieces of white construction paper with their name on it.

Be sure and have the children wear aprons to protect their clothes and have a pail of warm sudsy water to wash off the paint. Also be sure and talk about the colors and the texture of the fruits and vegetables while they are making the prints.

Watercolor Landscape

Take a small group of children outside while a helper watches the other children. The teacher will take watercolor sets, cups and clip-boards with watercolor papers attached to them. Tell the children to walk around with you, while they look at plants, trees and other outside nature things.

Then tell them to choose something that they have seen or currently see, that they would like to paint. Next pass out the materials for them to begin their painting. When the paintings are complete, bring the children and their pictures inside. Children will stay inside and play while the teacher takes out the next group. After everyone has had a turn painting and the paintings are dry, place all the pictures into a binder using plastic sheet protectors or hang them on the walls for all to see. Make sure each child's name is on their picture. If you choose to make the book, place it out on the counter so all can enjoy their new picture book.

Vegetable Stick Painting

Make a large carrot shape on thick or freezer paper. Children will use craft sticks to apply the paint. Place a small amount of shaving cream on carrot with a spoon of yellow and red poster paint. Now tell the children to mix the two paints with the shaving cream by using the stick. Ask them to guess what color it will make. Then they will spread the mixture over the carrot shape. Talk with children about what happened when the two different colors were mixed.

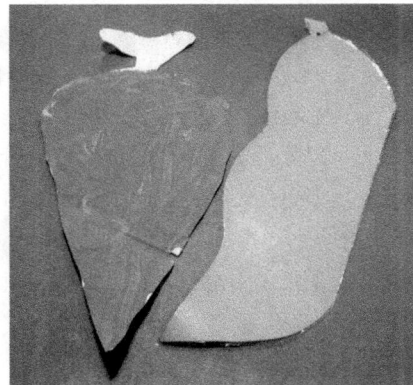

You can also do this activity using large pea pod shapes with colors blue and yellow. Have them mix colors again with the shaving cream. Another idea is to try using a large shape of a bunch of grapes with the colors blue, yellow and the shaving cream. Have fun mixing and reviewing how colors are made. See example.

Apple, Orange, or Lemon Tree

Provide large tracers of a top of a tree and tree trunks for the children to trace around. See example.

Children will trace the top of the tree onto light or dark green construction paper and the trunk on light or dark brown construction paper. Then they will cut around the edges and glue the trunk onto another piece of plain construction paper. Now they will cut out the tree top and glue it over the top part of the tree trunk.

Set out small plates with mixed red, orange or yellow paint on them. Children will choose one of colors and one of their fingers to dip into the paint and carefully make prints of the colored fruits on to their green tree top.

Flowers in a Row

Provide the children with a light blue, ivory or white piece of paper to use. Children can choose to have the paper in a horizontal or vertical position. Children will draw and cut green construction paper to make stems for their flowers. Have the children also draw several ovals or other shapes to represent leaves on the green paper. They will cut the stem and leaves out and glue them on to a large piece of watercolor paper. Demonstrate several ways they could glue the stem with the leaves and let them choose their own way to glue them. See example of stems and leaf.

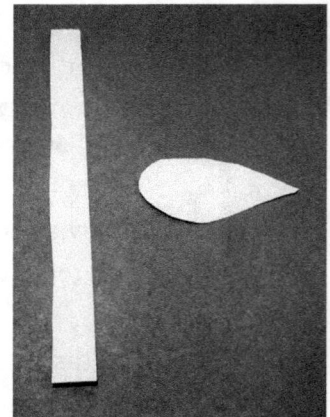

Now give them cupcake liner papers in small and regular sizes. They have a lot of bright colored ones and many different sizes in craft stores. The cupcake liners will be the tops of the flowers. They will choose the amount, size and colors to glue on the stems. If children want to add more things to their picture provide colored paper with scissors so they can create grass, clouds in the sky, a sun or even bugs.

Flower Necklace

Use a dye cut machine or other tool to cut out medium size flowers and punch holes in the middle of them. Then cut plastic drinking straws into 1 inch long pieces. Now cut lengths of yarn 28 inches long for each child in the class. Next either wrap one end of each piece of yarn with tape or put glue on one of the ends of the yarn and leave it to dry. Either of these methods will make it easier for the children to thread it through the straw pieces and the punch hole.

Have the children come to your table in small groups of four or five, so that you can help them if needed. It helps children to tape one end of the yarn to the table, so that the flowers and straws don't fall off the other end while still string straw pieces mixed with on. When they have completed with the number that the child wants, tie the two ends together for them to wear.

It would be good to show them pictures of Hawaiian leis that both men and women are wearing. This would let them know that both boys and girls wear them. Also talk with them about the friendship and greeting that is associated with the leis. Another time you can use silk flowers to make leis or use real flowers from home gardens if you have some that are suitable.

Lacing Trees

Use large poster board for the base part of your lacing cards. Make four cards from one large sheet by placing ends together evenly and fold it across the middle. Now fold it across the other way evenly. Then cut on the fold lines so that you will have four pieces the same size. Draw a simple tree on each piece of poster board and color inside your tree lines. Next, draw small colored apples (round circle) on the tree or other fruits such as peaches (oranges in color) or purple plums.

Now you will need a punch to make holes around the shape of the tree and then cover with clear contact paper on both sides. Then use the hole punch again in holes that have been covered. It is easier to punch it twice, than trying to punch it once through the poster board and the contact papers.

Teacher will provide long shoes laces for the children to lace the holes together or use a long piece of cording with the end taped. Children will lace in and out of the holes around the tree shape.

Vegetable Shapes

Draw simple outlines of vegetables on poster board and cut them out for children to use for tracers. Provide colored construction paper and pencils for children to trace the vegetables on and scissors to cut them out. Use the shapes they cut for a border on

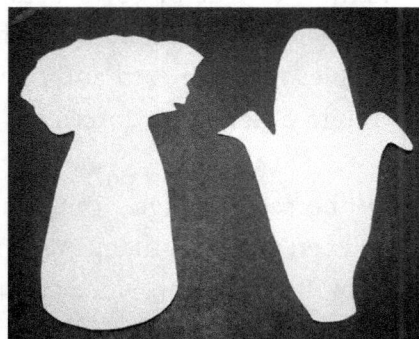

your bulletin board. Be sure and have their names showing, so everyone can admire their hard work! See example of patterns.

LANGUAGE AND LITERACY

Outside Collage

Take a few of the children for a short walk around the school and have them collect things like pine cones, leaves, wild flower weeds, small twigs and other nature things in a lunch size bag with their name on it. Make sure to have their name on their bags. Now let the children play in the classroom while a helper watches them. Now take the next small group outside and do the same thing with these children.

When all the children have had a turn collecting thing from outside, call them over to the table in small groups and have them make a collage of the items from their bag on heavy paper using glue. When the collages have been made in that small group, have the children each take turns telling about their collages to the other children in their group. You might ask questions to help them talk about their picture. An example would be to have them tell what the items are, why they choose them and how them decided to put them together. Do this with each small group. Then when all of the pictures are dry put them on display for all to see.

Fruit or Vegetable Bingo

Teacher will make five square cards on poster board. Then draw two columns down and two columns across each card. These will look like a tick tack toe cards. Then use computer to make fruits or veggies that will fit inside the columns. You could also use stickers from a school supple store or draw simple ones like a carrot, potato, peas in a pod, a head of lettuce, an ear of corn, a tomato, an egg plant, a stalk of celery and an onion. You will need nine of each set of vegetables for each card and one more of each vegetable for the bingo caller. Print copies of your veggies. See example.

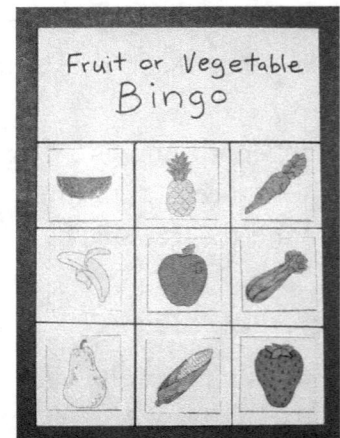

Glue one set of veggies onto each card. Place the veggies in different places on each card. Then laminate them. Also make a caller set and put them on squares and laminate. To play the game, provide each player with a card and nine tokens (such as buttons or beans) to cover the veggie that the caller names.

The caller will draw a caller card from a stack and show and say the name of the fruit or veggie.

Children in the small group will find the matching one on their card and cover it with a token. The first person or persons to notice their card is all covered says, "Bingo." They will then tell the caller the names of the veggies and fruits on their card to make sure that they really have bingo.

Watch children for signs of interest and when they are starting to lose interest, stop playing. Tell the children they can play the game again the next day. The next day have children take turns being the caller. This will help them learn the names of the fruits and vegetables.

Vegetable Categorizing

Use veggies from the garden and/or from the store for this game. Collect many different vegetables, so that you will have categories of color and textures. Take the veggies out of bags one at a time and place them on the table. Have the children name them and then talk about the different colors of each vegetable and its texture. Now have the children find ones that are the same color and put them into groups of similar colors. For example, different shades of red – strawberries, cherries and tomatoes. Tell them that they have found a group or category that represent "red fruits and vegetables."

Now ask them to find another group of fruit and vegetables that have a similar color. Example green group – lettuce, spinach, peas in a pod, green apples and green grapes. Then proceed as before by talking about how they formed a category of fruit and vegetables of similar color. Next do this with the color orange and proceed as before.

Now ask the children to group fruit and vegetables a new way. They may not use colors, but they can use the following: group sizes that are similar(big and small), textures that are similar (smooth and rough), similar shapes (round and oval). After they have decided what category they will look for, ask them how they will know if they belong together. Help them think through this process if they have trouble deciding. It will be easier to use sizes and later to use textures. They will learn how to classify and vocabulary words and meanings through this hands on activity.

Pot Lid Snatch Game

Children will each have items to be placed out in front of them. When teacher mentions an item they quickly place the correct item in front of them and the teacher tries to snatch it with the pot lid.

One example of the game uses different colors of yarn cut in 12 inch piece of colored yarn to represent snakes. Each child is given the yarn in the colors that you are reviewing or learning. Black, brown, gray and white are often colors that need reviewing. Tell the children that you will try and catch their snake. When the teacher says a color, the children will move that color of yarn like a snake in front of them and the teacher will try and catch as many as she can with the lid. They must use the color that the teacher mentioned. Play continues using different colors of snakes. When they can do this well, change the colors to different ones. Make sure they all have new sets of the colors to play the game.

You can also use this activity to learn shapes, letters and numbers. Make cards with the shapes, letters or numbers on them that you want the children to learn. Be sure and put them on long pieces of card stock so that you can catch them under the lid without getting their fingers. Then give each child two or more of the cards with the shape, letter or number on them. Play the game the same way as catching the snake. They love this game and learn a lot too.

Apple Worm Game

Purchase enough plastic apples for a small group to use. Five children at a time usually works best. Apples can be purchased at a craft store and sometimes at the dollar store. You will also need a rubber worm for each apple. You can buy these in the fishing supply part of stores such as Wal-Mart during spring/summer seasons or other sporting stores.

Teacher will give verbal directions of positional places for the children to place their worm using their apple as the place the worm will be positioned. This will help children to understand and use the words correctly: over, under, on top of, behind, in front of, beside. An example would be place your worm over the apple. You can also have the children put the worm between their fingers. Using the objects helps children understand positioning better when they hear directions. When they can do this, have them take turns giving the directions, but they must use their apple and worm to show and tell where the worm goes.

What Goes Together

Assemble garden gloves, hand garden tools such as small digger & rake, small watering container, potting soil, seeds, knee pads and a number of other items that do not go together such as toy cars, hair brush, crayons, keys and other items.

Have the small group sitting around the table and show two items to the children that go together and one item that does not go with the other two items. Teacher will take turns asking a child which items go together and which do not. Then have the child tell why they go together and why not. Continue taking turns using different items with different children. This will help the children learn vocabulary and classification skills.

FREE TIME

CREATIVE ARTS

It is best to let children do creative projects on their own as much as possible. Children then can experience the fun of "doing" their projects. What they produce may not look perfect, but they enjoy the process of "doing" more than the actual completed project. Use words like, "I like that green color. It looks interesting the way you made that design with your brush." Rather than saying, "that picture is pretty or it looks like tree to me."

Teachers should also help children to say positive things about other children's projects. When children say something like, "That's not how a tree looks." You could say all tress are different and he can draw it the way he wants it to look." Be sure and teach skills, such as cutting at a different time than when they are creating. When they are creating, don't criticize their skills. Just make a note to work on that skill at a different time.

Make sure that each project includes the child's name somewhere on it, so that he/she can show others what he/she made. When teacher wants to write the words of the child that goes with the project, get permission before writing on it. If the child doesn't want you to write on it, write his or her words on a sticky note to go with the project. Also, let the children know where to place their project to dry and where they can display their project when dry.

New Ways of Finger Painting

Use freezer paper, finger paint paper or any paper with a glazed surface. For paint you can use powdered tempera mixed with liquid dish soap or mix it with saving cream. You can also use pudding or Jello mixed with liquid soap or shaving cream. You can use vanilla instant pudding mixed with milk and then chilled. You can also use the vanilla pudding mixed with food coloring to create many different colors or use different flavors to create different colors.

Provide aprons for each child and have a pail with warm sudsy water for them to raise off hands before going to sink to finish cleaning their hands.

Choose the type of paint and paper to use for your painting and let children help mix it. Tell them to have fun making different designs with their fingers. Also tell them that they can make a print of their picture by placing a clean sheet of paper over their design and smoothing it down. Then tell them to lift it off carefully to see their print.

Sprinkled Painting

Provide paper, small glue bottles, salt shakers with glitter in them, trays and bowls. Children will place aprons on to protect their clothing and write their name on the back of their paper. Then they will use glue to create what they want on the paper.

Next they will place their paper onto a tray. Now they will sprinkle the glitter onto their paper. Next they will turn their paper upside down on a tray. Then dump tray glitter into bowl. Now place their glitter paper on the counter to dry.

Blot Prints

Provide paper that has been folder in half and poster paint in a squeeze bottle such as a mustard container. Prepare several colors. Children will come to the table and drop paint onto their open paper. Then they will fold closed again and smooth it out with their hand. Next open paper and discover their design. They can make more than one design. They may want to try different ways to place their paint to mix colors or make different designs.

String Painting

Teacher will supply large water color sheets folded in half. Small plates with mixed paint and 12 inch pieces of yarn or string. Tell the children to use the string to create a picture. They may dip it into paint and move it around on the outside of the folded paper, place it between the folded paper and move it around, pull it through the folded paper or use it to print their picture by putting it between the sheets and pressing down on the top sheet. They could then take the string off and see their pictures. Encourage them to use the string in as many ways as they can think of to make pictures. Have them share the different pictures that they made with others.

SENSORY

Pretend Planting Table

Place potting soil, small hand shoves, flower pots and artificial flowers, small gardening gloves and vines with the table or pails. Children can pretend to plant the vines and flowers in the pots.

Soil Fun

Set out real soil in a small pail with a large spoon and small spray bottles of water. Also place small bowls with spoons for children to mix soil with sprayed water. Have card stock paper nearby so children can put some of their mixture on it if they want to. You could also have a small pail of sand that they could add to the mixture and she the difference it makes to their mixture. Children love this activity and will spend a lot of time mixing. Be sure and have them wear aprons and wash their hands well after this activity.

Sand

Buy water mills and an outdoor toy area during warm weather and use them all year long. They work well with sand or water. Place several in a sensory table with scoops to pour sand into the top of the mill causing it to spin. You could also place one in a pail for one child to use at a time. Children could sign their name on a piece of paper that is close to the area so they can have a turn without standing in line waiting. Use a timer for the children using the water\sand mill, so that they will know when their time is up. Be sure to monitor it. The children cross off their name when their turn starts. You can also use bird seeds instead of the sand or water. They always enjoy the mills.

DRAMATIC PLAY & SOCIAL DEVELOPMENT

Flower Shop

Set out materials such as artificial flowers\ greenery, vases, flower pots with florist foam in them, small tables for the to use as counters, toy cash registers, play money, paper cut in long strips for receipts, pencils, play phones, aprons for the workers, dress-up clothes for the customers, bags for their purchases, poster boards with markers to make signs for the store, small squares of paper to write prices for the items, tape, small chairs, paper for writing of draw pictures of what they are ordering, folded paper to make cards to go with the plants\flowers, crayons. Encourage the children to take turns using the most popular items in their shop. If that doesn't work use necklaces made from a yarn with a paper flower strung on it. Children would need to wear a necklace to use the popular item. Teacher will limit their time and give it to the next child on a list to use it.

Vegetable/Fruit Stand

Set out as many of these props as you can: small tables for counter, shelve units for the foods, use plastic fruits and vegetables (real sturdy ones like carrots and apples or a combination of them), cash register, play money, dress up clothes for customers, aprons and hats for the workers, purses and wallets, paper to make receipts and orders with pencils, bags, poster boards with markers for signs, tape. Use necklaces as in the flower shop for popular features.

SCIENCE

Place seeds with pictures of what grows from them and magnifying glasses for children to use on the science table. Also place by a window a large holed sponge that has been soaked in water into a small cake pan. Have the children help sprinkle grass seeds on top of it. Children will observe to see how seeds grow. When the grass gets tall let the children take turns carefully use scissors to trim it. Then watch it grow again. Keep a small water spray bottle nearby to keep it moist.

Another idea to use is to place a potato on a shallow bowl and add a little water to the container to watch it grow. Soon it will begin to sprout roots and if left long enough, stems and leaves. You can show and point out the different parts of the plant. You can plant it in a large pail and then it will produce small flowers and if you pollinate it, small potatoes will grow under the soil. The potatoes start growing after the flowers have been pollinated. When they have had time to grow you can remove it from the pail to let the children examine it.

Another fun thing to do is to place a stock of celery in a clear glass of water and add red food coloring to it. It works best if you use a stock of celery with leaves on it and let it sit for a little while for it to get a little limp before placing it in the colored water. The water travels quicker up the stock that way. You can also use blue in the water, but it is harder to see it in the stock and leaves. Then you can ask the children how they think the red made the leaves and stock red. Then relate that to how water travels in plants.

Planting Activity

Supply foam cups, medium sized nail, potting soil, large spoons, watering can or measuring cup with spout, bean or radish seeds and permanent colored markers. Children will place several small holes in the bottom of their cups. Then they will put on aprons to protect their clothing and carefully use the colored markers to decorate their cup and write their name on it.

Next they will move to a table that has a pail of the potting soil on it and they will spoon soil into their cup. Soil should be about an inch from the top. Children will then place two bean seeds about ¾ of an inch to 1 inch under the soil and water it. If using radish seeds, have the children place seeds barely under the soil and water them. Both beans and radish seeds are easy to grow. Now children will place the cups on a tray with sides by a window. The holes in the cups will help the seeds from getting too much water. Only water the seeds when the soil is dry.

Place sheets of paper nearby and each day have a child draw a line down so that they can keep track of how long the seeds have been planted. Have them make guesses to see how many days they think the first seed will start to grow. Record each child's name and their guess near the tallying sheet. Tell them that they are scientists because scientists make guesses to learn about things too. When the seeds start to sprout have them look at their guesses to see if they got close to the number of days. Ask them what they learned about seeds and plants.

Fruits

Have children gather round the science table as you cut open a few different fruits such as an apple, orange, lemon, pear, peach or watermelon. Talk about the parts of the fruits – skin, fruit, seeds and or pits. Then have them look at the color, texture, smell and size. Then offer small samples of the fruits and talk about the different tastes of the fruits. Ask them to guess why the fruits have seeds in them. Plant some of the seeds to see what will happen. Place books about the different fruits around the table. Make sure the books are age appropriate and have lots of pictures. You can find book in the junior non-fiction books in your local library.

48

GROSS MOTOR SKILLS

Pass the Vegetables

Select and line up two or more teams of children. It is best to have about six children in each team, so they don't stand around doing nothing for long periods of time. Have the teams stand next to each other, but not too close. Use hardy vegetables such as winter squash, potatoes or small pumpkins for the children to pass in this activity.

Children will stand in two lines and pass between their legs the pumpkin (or other vegetable) to the child behind them. When the last person in their line receives the pumpkin they will pass it over their head to the person in front of them. When the pumpkin is at the front again have them pass it back to the end of the line between their legs and sit down. Each team will try to be the first ones to sit down.

Fruit Push

Make a line with masking tape for each them to follow. Put some curves in it and have it about 25 feet long and then it will turn and go back the where it started. Children will be placed into two or more teams. Each team will be given a fruit such as an apple, orange or lemon. They will sit in a line and until the game begins.

Then first person in each team will then get down on hands and knees and follow the masking tape line for their team by pushing with their head the fruit that has been placed on the floor by the teacher. When the have followed it back to the start, they will go to the back of their line and stand up and next person at the front of the line will follow the tape by pushing the fruit. As soon as the teams complete the course and are standing up they will say all together "Yea! Yea! We Pushed Our Best." Then they sit down and watch the others finish and cheer.

Action Song

Sing to the tune "The Farmer in the Dell" things that the farmer could do to grow food. Example:

> The farmer plants the seeds,
>
> The farmer plants the seeds,
>
> Hi O the Dairy O,
>
> The farmer plants the seeds.

While singing the song the children act out the action of planting the seeds (bending over and placing seeds in the ground). The farmer could water the seeds (spray water), pull up the weeds (bend over and pull), harvest the potatoes (dig with the shovel), eats the food (pretend eating), sells the food (loading it in the truck and drive it to market). Have fun singing and moving with the song. The children can help you add verses too.

FIELD TRIP IDEAS

Look in the phone book for a garden store or nursery that may be nearby and make arrangement to visit them. Ask if they could show and tell the children about their business and the plants they have. Explain to them that they are studying plants and would like to see their green houses and see how they grow plants. Ask if they have any small inexpensive plants that your class could buy to take to their homes and plant.

If there are no places close then ask parents if they have gardens or know of someone that has gardens that the children could go and see and learn about. If you can go don't forget to get permission from all the parents and help from them on the trip. Take important permission forms and emergency forms for each child, a first aid kit and a cell phone. Also take a small snack with water for the children. Another important thing to do before you leave is have the children make thank you cards for the business or people's garden you are visiting.

Earth Week

GROUP ACTIVITIES/CIRCLE TIME

MUSIC AND MOVEMENT

"Big Beautiful Planet" Tape from Raffi Rise and Shine by Raffi with Ken Whiteley.

"A- Camping We Will Go" Tape from Barney's Favorites Vol. 1.

"And The Green Grass Grows All Around" Tape from Barney's Favorites Vol. 1. This is a fun song to act out while singing.

"The Sharing Song" Tape from Raffi Singable Songs for the Very Young. This song helps teach children to be kind to each other.

"Down by the Bay" Tape from Raffi Singable Songs for the Very Young.

"Baby Beluga" tape from Baby Beluga by Raffi.

"We All Live Together" from We All Live Together Vol. 1 CD/Tape by Greg & Steve.

"The World Is a Rainbow" from We All Live Together Vol. 2 CD/Tape by Greg & Steve. This song helps teach children that it does not matter what color your skin is or where you come from, you are all special in your own ways.

"The World Family" from Kiss Your Brain CD by Dr. Jean.

"Hooray For The World" from Teaching Peace CD by Red Grammer, Atcha Music, Inc.

"It's A Small World" from CD "Five Little Monkeys by Kimbo Educational.

The following songs are found on the tape "Our Earth" from "Macmillian Sing & Learn Program" from Newbridge Communication, Inc. They offer great songs that are just right for preschool age children. The songs are presented in ways that allow the children to use movements and actions without having heard or practiced them the songs.

Side 1 "Greetings, World!

   "Join Hands"
   "Cleanup Kangaroo"
   "Swimming in the Sea"
   "Growing Plants"
   "Air, Air Everywhere"

Side 2 "The Butterfly"

   "Betsy Baker's Boat"
   "Moon Play"
   "Rock, Water, and Air"
   "All Around the World"
   "A Wonderful Place"

You can also use any of the children favorite songs they enjoy with this lesson.

LANGUAGE AND LITERACY

All the Colors of the Earth by Sheila Hamanaka, Scholastic Inc.

Long Live Earth by Meighan Morrison, Scholastic Inc.

Earth by Melvin and Gilda Berger, Scholastic Inc.

Sun and Moon by Marcus Pfister, Scholastic Inc.

What The Sun Sees, What The Moon Sees by Nancy Tafuri, Scholastic Inc.

You're Aboard Spaceship Earth by Patricia Lauber and illustrated by Holly Keller, Scholastic Inc.

The Moon by Melvin and Gilda Berger, Scholastic Inc.

Watching the Sun by Edana Eckart, Scholastic Inc.

Watching the Moon by Edana Eckart, Scholastic Inc.

The Solar System by Melvin and Gilda Berger, Scholastic Inc.

The Sun by Melvin and Gilda Berger, Scholastic Inc.

The Earth and I by Frank Asch, Scholastic Inc.

Franklin Plants A Tree based on characters created by Paulette Bourgeois and Brenda Clark, Scholastic Inc.

Earth Dance by Joanne Ryder and illustrated by Norman Gorbaty, Scholastic Inc.

The Family of Earth by Schim Schimmel, Scholastic Inc.

Let's Take Care of the Earth by Rozanne Lanczak Williams and illustrated by Neena Chawla, Creative Teaching Press Inc.

The Great Trash Bash by Loreen Leedy, Scholastic Inc.

Earth Day Hooray! by Stuart J. Murphy and illustrated by Renee Andriani, Scholastic Inc.

Trashy Town by Andrea Zimmerman and David Clemesha, Scholastic Inc.

Reduce, Reuse, Recycle by Rozanne Lanczak Williams and illustrated by Neena Chawla, Creative Teaching Press Inc.

Recycle Every Day! by Nancy Elizabeth Wallace, Scholastic Inc.

Pebbles And Pods: A Book of Nature Crafts by Goldie Taub Chernoff with pictures by Margaret Hartelius, Scholastic Inc.

Diary of A Worm by Doreen Cronin with pictures by Harry Bliss, Scholastic Inc.

Be a Friend to Trees by Patricia Lauber and illustrated by Holly Keller, Scholastic Inc.

Archaeologists Dig For Clues by Kate Duke, Scholastic Inc.

Danny and the Dinosaur Go to Camp by Syd Hoff, Scholastic Inc.

Monk Camps Out by Emily Arnold McGully, Scholastic Inc.

Pig Pig Goes to Camp by David McPhail, Scholastic Inc.

Baby Beluga by Raffi and illustrated by Ashley Wolff, Crown Publishers, Inc., a Random House Company.

Where Does All the Garbage Go? by Melvin Berger, Newbridge Communications, Inc.

I like to have children think about the things that are beautiful all around us. The mountains, grassy hills, the sunrise and set, the moon in its different phases, the water flowing from a little stream into a large river and making its way into a large lake or ocean are a few of the things I want the children to take notice of. One way to do this is through reading good books to them.

Then after children become aware of their soundings, introduce them to caring for the world around them. This could include the how different people's actions can help the earth and the animals that live on it. Then children could consider how their actions effect the earth and what they can do to keep it beautiful in their home and community. I hope these books can help you do that. Be sure an check your local library for these books and additional ones.

SMALL GROUP ACTIVITIES/TABLE TIMES

MATH & COGNITIVE

Recycle Math Game

Ask each parent to save a clean egg carton for their child to use in a recycling project. Tell parents early so that they have time to obtain one. Give a date for them to send the carton to school. Tell the parents that the class will be talking about recycling and taking care of the earth. You can also ask parents to help with scraps of materials to decorate the cartons. Some of the items they could help with are pieces of felt, material scraps, leftover stickers, leftover sequins, ribbons or pieces of crepe paper, buttons or any other materials they have on hand for the children to decorate their egg cartons. Supply whatever else you can from the classroom.

Provide glue, markers, a small plastic bag with five beans inside it for each child and prepared 1 inch squares. The squares will each need to have a different number on them or a shape depending on the needs of each child. Teacher will type up the directions for the game for the parent's information.

Example of note shown.

> Dear Mom and Dad,
>
> Please play this game with me. I made it. It will be fun and I can practice saying my numbers and shape names after I shake the box (with the lid closed). I will say the name of the shape or number where the beans land to you.
>
> Thanks for playing with me!

Children will glue in the bottom of each egg cup a paper square with the number or shape right side up. They will also write their name on their carton. Next they will use the materials you have prepared to decorate their egg carton.

Play the game several times with each child when their carton is dry. After playing the game have children place the note and beans in their plastic bag and place it in their egg carton. Tell the children to take the game home and play it with their Mom, Dad or another older child. Tell them to have parents let you know how their child did playing the game. See example.

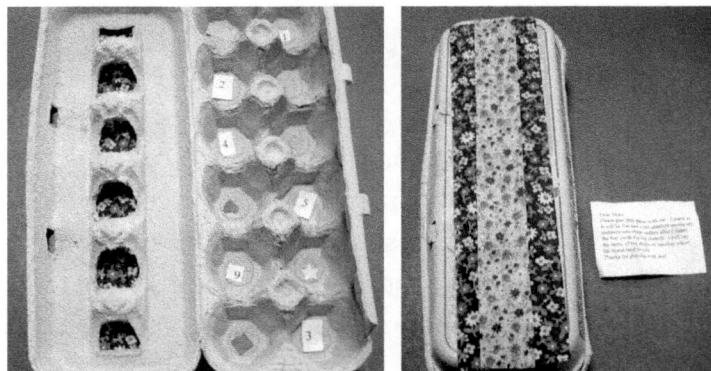

Magic Cups

Collect and save clean, used plastic margarine tubs, plastic lids, drinking cups and other plastic clean containers that usually are discarded. Have the parents help you save these items. Tell them that they need to be washed for this recycling project. Teacher will need hole punches and or nails with hammers for the children to make a hole in each plastic item and 6 inch pieces of yarn.

You will need a toaster oven or regular oven and cookie sheets that have been covered with foil. Also provide colored permanent markers for the children to decorate the plastic containers. Make sure they write their names on the cups.

Discuss with the children that we can reuse things that would normally go in the trash. Discuss different things that could be recycled such as collecting paper for the recycle bin and other things that could be reused. Tell them that today they will be making decorations for the classroom. Show them the items that have been collected. Tell them that we will discover what will happen to the containers and the lids. Children will decorate them with the markers and place a hole in them.

Children will place the completed item on top of a foil lined cookie sheet. Teacher will preheat the to 350 degrees. Then when the oven is warm enough have the children watch through the oven window while the items shrink on the foil. If no window to watch just have them view items before and after placing them in the oven. When the items are cool have them string the yarn pieces through the hole and help them tie it. Now they can be hung up around the classroom. Have them notice that the clear ones let the light shine through. They would look good on the window to catch the sun light. See example.

Bird Feeders

This project is ideal for the winter months when birds are looking for food sources. Collect pine cones in the fall and save them for this project. Or if you don't live near mountains, try finding pine trees at parks. You can buy the scented cones at Christmas time and use them at home or in the class while they smell good. Then save them to reuse when the scent is gone for this project. Also watch for sales on cheap peanut butter and bird seed.

Discuss with the children that when the grounds are covered with snow it's hard for the birds to find food. Talk about how we could help them by reusing pine cones to make feeders for them. Tell the children that we will tie pieces of yarn onto pine cones so we can hang them on trees. Then they will use plastic knives to spread the peanut butter on the cones. Now they will roll the pine cones on a cookie sheet that has bird seeds placed on it. When the cones are all completed have them go outside with you to hang them in the trees or other place off the ground.

Have children check the area often to see what colors of birds eat the seeds. Have them take small clip boards with pencils outside to draw what they see. A clean garbage lid could also be used for a bird bath. Children could be assigned different days to place clean water in it. Have a book in your classroom with pictures of birds from your area for the children to look for and learn about.

Caring For Animals

Purchase small plastic animals such as farm, pet or other animals to use with this activity. Place the animals in a bag and bring one animal out at a time and ask children to think of different things the animal needs to be healthy. Continue bringing out one animal at a time and having children tell ways to care for the animal. Then have the children help you place them in one line and count them.

Next have the children sort the animals by color, type or any other way that makes sense and children can easily see how they would go together. Now have the children tell you which group has the most and the least animals. If they don't know which group is more or less than the other ones have them count each group and then decide. Find another way to sort them and find out again which group is the most or less.

Shape Find

Prepare cards using pictures of shapes you would like children to learn this week. Copy the cards so that each child in your small group has one. Then have the children sit in a circle with you and call out a shape name that is on the cards such as a circle. Tell everyone to point to that shape on their card and say its name. Continue in the same manor until you have said each shape name.

Now say each shape name again, but this time have the children say something about each shape. They could say things such as, "This shape has two long and two short sides. It's a rectangle." Another example would be, "This circle shape is like a ball." Help the children figure out how to describe the shape with questions such as "How many sides does it have?"

Then on another day review the descriptions of the shapes with the cards. When you feel they know how to describe the shapes, tell them that they are going outside with you. They will use the cards to help them find shapes in nature and things they see around them. When they have found a shape on their card they should say, "I found one." Then they should describe it for the other children, so they can see it too. When all the children in the small group have found at least one shape and described it you can go back inside. You can use it again another day.

Sparkle Bottles

Save and clean water bottles for each child in your class. Buy or use your glitter for this project. Also buy a bag of craft beads. If your children need to learn how many things equal different numbers, pick a small number such as 5, a medium number such as 10 or a large number such as 20 to work on. Each child can work on the same number or different numbers.

Children will put their name on their water bottle and put water in it close to the top of the bottle. Then they go a table that has the glitter on it. Place the bowls on trays, so that the surplus glitter can be saved. Place the glitter in small bowls. Have the children place the funnels in the bottle and then scoop one spoon of the glitter into their bottle.

Next have them go to the next area to count the beads to place into their bottle. The number of beads depends on them being able to count and place the beads in a line while counting them correctly. You may want to limit them to a certain number such as 20 or use smaller number for those having difficulty with counting them. Write their number on the bottle with a permanent marker or have them write it. Now have them put a ring of glue around the top of the bottle where it screws on. Then screw the lid on tightly and let it dry. After it has dried they can shake it and recount the beads inside it.

FINE MOTOR SKILLS

Colorful Earth

Prepare a circle that will fit into a paper plate. Then use a picture of the earth's continents to draw the land masses on the circle. See example. Now copy your circle the amount of times so that each child can have a copy and save a copy for your file. Purchase a small bottle of clear corn syrup, paper plates and have blue and green food coloring on hand. Teacher will mix small amounts of corn syrup with blue coloring and with the green coloring.

Find a picture on the internet or library that shows the earth from space. You will use this picture to point out that the water from space appears to be blue and the land areas with plants and trees spears to be green. Tell the children that they will be making a picture of how the earth looks from space.

Children will use their cutting skills to cut out their circle. Then they will glue the earth picture onto the center of their plate. Then they will use the corn two colors or corn syrup with a small brush to paint in the earth picture. Also caution them to use only a thin layer of the colors so they will dry faster. Be sure and have them write their names on the plate. The plates will need to be laid flat to allow them to dry completely. When they have dried children will punch a hole at the top and thread a piece of yarn through it. Teacher may have to help them tie it. Now hang them up around the classroom. It will be shinny when dry.

Light Catchers

For this recycle project ask parents to help you collect old or advertisement CDs. When you have one for each child, do the activity. You will need pencils, scissors, white card stock paper, fishing line, glue and colored markers.

Children will place the CD on the card stock paper and trace around it with a pencil. Then they will cut out their circle and glue it onto the CD side that does not have the data/rainbows. Then they will make their own designs on the paper side. When they are through drawing, have them use their pencil to make a hole. The hole should be in the center of the paper where the hole of the CD is located. They now can thread the fishing line through hole and tie it. Hang it near a window of by a light and see the rainbow effect it will make from the shinny side of the CD. See example.

Rhythm Containers

Save tubes that chips come in, oatmeal boxes, drink bottles or any other containers that have a lids. Make sure they are clean. Buy small bags of beans and/or rice. Children will decorate their container by using markers, stickers or cutting their own designs from colored construction paper and gluing them on their containers.

Next have them place beans, rice or a combination of the two inside their tube or container. They will shake it gently to hear the sound that it makes. Have them tell you if the sound is loud or soft. Then they can change its sound by changing what is in it. For example, beans give a loud sound and rice a softer sound in containers. When they like their sound have them glue the lid on. Make sure they have their name on it and wait for the lid to dry.

Now put on a music CD and have them shake it to the rhythm of the beat in the songs played. Encourage them to share instruments with their friends to hear and enjoy the sounds that each container makes.

Lacing Cards

Buy some lacing cards to help them develop finger strength or make your own. When making your own cards use thick poster board or go to a hardware store and purchase shop board that has holes in it to use for hanging tools. They are sturdy and will last for a long time. Paint a simple tree on a square of the board and supply a shoelace for the children to lace around.

The poster board can also be cut into squares. Then draw simple nature shapes such as a large flower with petals and make holes around the flower with a hole punch or large nail. Then provide a long shoelace to sew around the shape. You can also use a piece of yarn to sew with if you tape the ends of the yarn.

You can also have the children design their own square of poster board and make the holes around it with a large nail. Use a piece of Styrofoam under their square and let them pound a large nail through the picture into the Styrofoam to make the holes around their picture. They will enjoy sew around their own pictures.

Earth Day Badge

Make a badge pattern like the example on card stock. Make five or six of them so that children at your small group can each use one. They will need pencils, markers, crayons, scissors, small gems from the craft store and glue.

They will trace around badge pattern with a pencil and then cut out their badge. Teacher will have slips printed with the words Earth Day on them. Each child will need one to glue onto their badge.

Have markers and crayons available for children to decorate their badge. Also provide small gems from the craft store for them to glue onto their badge. Have the children lay the completed badge flat until dry. Then attach a piece of rolled masking tape to the back of the badge so they can press it on to their clothes so they can wear them on Earth Day.

Marble Painting

For this activity you will need: several shallow boxes or lids with sides, large and small marbles and or small jack balls or golf balls, long size watercolor paper, poster paint in several colors, child aprons and pencils.

Children will put their name on a piece of paper and then place it in the lid or box with their name side facing down. Now have them put on an apron and select several colors of paint. Help them, if needed place several small globs of each color of paint on their paper. Then have them choose a few balls and place them on top of their paper.

Tell them to carefully roll the balls back and forth across the paint on their paper. Encourage them to tip the box slowly and keep balls inside of the box/lid. Ask them what is happening to the paint. Also have them guess what may happen if they continue to roll the ball into a different color and then back into their original color. When they are finished have them place their paintings on a flat surface to dry. This project helps them develop control as they move the balls back and forth without telling the balls fall out of the box/lid.

Sand Painting

Supply small glue bottles, pencils, large trays and card stock or pieces of cardboard that has been cut to size. The cardboard pieces can be used as is or they can be covered with foil. The sand used can be some that you have collected, bought or you can make salt look like sand. The cardboard pieces work best and give the paintings more support.

Making different colors of salt with tempera paint is simple. Just mix powdered tempera paint with the salt. Powder can be found in art supplies or at school supply store. It is an economical way to make wet paint too and mixes instantly with water when you want wet paint. You can also use dry Jello to make colored salt. Just mix different flavors to obtain different colors of salt.

Start by having children write their names or the back of their paper or cardboard. Then have them draw small lines of glue across their paper/cardboard to create designs. Next have them place their paper/cardboard on a tray and sprinkle it with one color of sand. Then they will tip up their design carefully and sand will fall on the tray. Next tip tray over bowl to catch the sand. Now they can choose a different color to sprinkle over their paper/cardboard making sure it is in the tray. Then tip extra sand off onto tray and tip tray sand into bowl as before. Continue to add sand on glue until child is through.

Let dry laying flat and when it is dry you can add yarn to hang pictures around room. Using the glue bottles to make small lines increases small muscle control in fingers. Tipping the picture and tray also helps develop coordination.

Recycle Bag

Ask parents to help you save clean paper grocery bags and send them to school. You may also have them save appropriate magazines for the children to cut. When the items have been collected, assemble them together and set out the scissors, and markers. Make a few words strips with the word recycle written on them.

Children will write their names on a bag and write the word recycle by copying the word. If more help is needed write the word recycle written on their bag with a pencil and have them trace it with a marker. Next pass out the scissors, magazines and bottles of glue. Tell children to cut out the pictures that they like to decorate their bag and glue them on the outside of their bag.

When the bags are dry send them home with the children. They can collect things for school in them like empty tubes, clean water bottles and magazines or whatever their parents would like them to collect to recycle.

Nail Boards

Purchase soft wood scraps from a lumber department. Have the wood cut into appropriate sizes for children to use. Also purchase eye goggles for children and nails with a large heads that are about 2 inches long. If you can, borrow or buy four or five hammers for this small group.

Teach the children safety rules for the use of hammers such as always wear the safety goggles when using the hammer and hold nail away from the top of the nail. Now demonstrate how to pound the nail into the wood and let them try to do it one at a time with you. Next stay close by and have them try it on their own. This is a very good activity to develop coordination and motor skills.

Sock Puppets

Ask parents to help save socks that they longer use because one is missing or children outgrew. Tell them that they will be using them to make puppets. If you don't get enough socks for the children, buy some at the dollar store. Each pair will give you two socks to use. Also collect buttons, scraps of material, wiggle eyes, fuzzy wire pieces, feathers and anything else that would help the children make a puppet.

Have glue and scissors on hand for children to use to make their puppet. They can make a person or an animal. You can also include yarn for hair. Provide thick pieces of paper to place inside the socks so that children won't glue the opening closed. Be sure and show the children how the sock fits on a hand, so that they won't make it upside down. Now let them cut, glue and create their own puppet. Be sure and have their names written on them using a fine tip marker or a piece of tape attached to them with their name. See example.

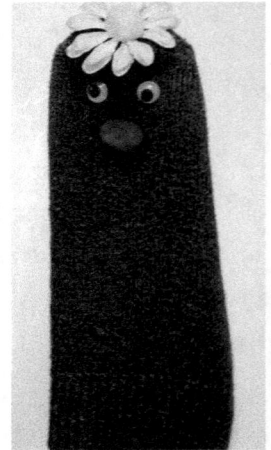

LANGUAGE AND LITERACY

Caring for the Earth

You will need to provide each child a small bag and disposable gloves for this activity. Tell the children that we are going to go outside and clean up the play ground. The items can be picked up with the gloves and placed in their bags. Caution the children not to pick up glass or anything that might hurt them, but to show you anything that might not be safe, so that you can dispose of it safely.

Give the children time to pick a few things each. Then take them inside and talk about the items found that each child found. Ask them how it felt to help clean up the yard. Also ask what they could do to take of their play yard. Ask them what they could do if another child threw their garbage on the ground. Have the children role play different things that they could do when others don't put their trash away. Tell them that they did an important job in keeping the earth clean. Ask what they could do at home and in the car to keep the earth clean. Thank them for their help.

Then take another group out and continue until all the children in your class have had an opportunity to participate in cleaning up and in the discussions and role playing. Be sure and recognize each child that helped.

Fishing for a Letter

Buy a dowel stick at a craft store and tie a 20 inch piece of yarn at the end of the stick. Then tape around the yarn so the yarn won't move on the stick. Now tie a strong magnet on the other end of the yarn. Make a simple fish pattern such as the one in the example and trace it onto colored foam sheets. Then cut the fish out and draw an eye on each fish and a letter with a permanent marker. You can make one for each letter in the alphabet. Next decide which letters are most important for the children in your small groups to learn. The first letter of each of the children names is a good place to start. Attach a large paper clip to each fish, so that the magnet will be able to pick up the fish that it comes in contact.

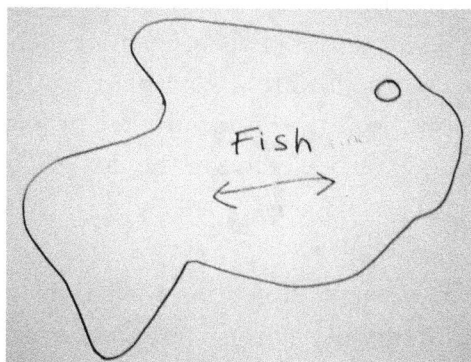

Use a sensory table, pail or a small wading pool to place the desired fish. Place a little water in it so the fish will float. Have four or five children come with the same number of fish. Have the children each take a turn of pulling a fish out. Then help the children to say the name of the letter that is on each fish that is caught. Next have them make the sound of the letter and try to name which child's name sounds like that letter. Help them if needed my sounding out each child's name that is in your small group. Next have another child who is the group fish out a letter and the group again says the letter name and sound made by that letter. Help them again by sounding out each child's name in the group. Continue as before until all the children have had a turn at your group.

Another time do this activity again and use different groups of children together. Continue playing this game on different days and over time they will recognize the letters of their class names and the sound the letters make. Then you can add the rest of the letters of the alphabet a little at a time.

Where's the Bee?

Buy plastic insects or make small bees using fuzzy wire wraps to form bees body, adding cut foam wings with fuzzy pipe cleaner antennas. Each child in the small group will need a bee and an artificial flower or use picture of bee and flower. See example.

Teacher will give directions during this activity using prepositions so children will learn the meaning of on, over, around, between, in front, behind and under. Examples: "Children put your bee over your flower." "Now place your bee behind your flower." "Make your bee fly around your flower." "Place your bee on your flower." "Place your bee in front of your flower." "Place your bee between the flower pedals." "Then place the bee under your flower."

Children will follow your movement directions with their bee and flower while you say the directions. Next children will say the directions with you while following your directions. Now children will take turns telling other children the movement directions while showing them what to do. Everyone should have a turn saying movement directions while showing others what to do.

Then practice with the children using their bodies to follow directions. Have them line up one behind the other and then have them move to standing in front of their chair. Next have them stand between two chairs and then go around their chair. Do this several times.

Name That Color

Play this game as a review, not when they are first learning their colors. Use colored construction squares of the basic colors for this game. You will also need two bells for the game. Use a chalkboard with chalk to keep score or a paper with marker.

Place the children into two teams and each team will stand in a line. The first person in each line will hold a bell and ring it as soon as they can say the name of a color shown.

The first person to ring their bell will say the name of the color. If they answer correctly their team earns one point. If they didn't say it correct the first person on the other team will say the color. If the second team says it correct they get the point. Then both players move to the back of the line and the new first team players hold the bells. Play continues as before with team members moving to the end of their line after their turn is over. Play continues until one team scores ten points.

Name That Farm Animal

You will need pictures of farm animals to play this game. Go through all the pictures with the children before playing the game, so that they all can review what the names of the farm animals. Now divide the children into two teams and two lines to play the game. If you have lots of children use more teams so that the lines aren't too long. Give each first person in the line a bike horn to squeeze when they know the answer. If you don't have horns, use rubber duck to squeeze for the sound or other device that would be fun for them to use.

Now play the game the same way as the game "Name That Color," but continue keeping score until the first team scores 20 points. Give all the players of both teams a few animal crackers after the game is over. Have fun learning and reviewing farm animal names.

Recycle Game

Bring various items such as an empty can, used water bottle, jeans with holes, doll with broken arm, toy car with missing wheel, a banana peeling, shirt with missing button, old news papers, old book, too small clothing and other items. Or cut out pictures from magazines or make small drawings and mount on squares pictures of various items.

Place either the items in a box or bag or the pictures in a small container. Have the children take turns picking one item and showing it to the others. Then have them think of ways that they could reuse the item by telling how it could be fixed of used in some other way. They can have other children in the class help them by calling on others. This will get them thinking and speaking because of the open ended questions.

FREE TIME

CREATIVE ARTS

Wood Sculptures

Obtain scraps of lumber from a hardware store, wood craft store or by permission from a construction site. Also you will need to buy wood glue or use regular white glue for children to use at the table. It is a good idea to use trays for children to work on so the projects can be moved to dry or you can use cut pieces of cardboard instead.

Children will decide what additional materials they want to use to create. They might want to use markers, paint with brushes or other items. Encourage children to get the items needed from your center of creative materials and supplies. Remind them to put their names of their item or on the cardboard that their art work is at. Let them enjoy the processes by giving them the time they need without hurrying them. Let they know if they do need more time to finish that they can keep working on it the next day or until it has been completed. Give comments on their work by using nonjudgmental statements such as, "I like the way you are working to get that piece of wood just where you want it."

Rock Painting

Have children bring a rock from home or collect rocks from your or neighbor's yard. If you live close to a construction site you could ask for permission to collect some rocks. You want rocks to be about 3-6 inches long. You can also buy some from a landscaping company. You will need at least one for each child and a couple of extra ones so that they can have a choice. When you have the rocks have the children help prepare them for painting by washing the rocks and placing them on newspapers to dry.

Assemble aprons, poster paint in several colors with big and little paint brushes for the table where they will be working. Next put out the paint materials, rocks, and containers of clean water, to clean their brushes when changing colors.

Also provide pieces of cut cardboard for the children to place their rock and a marker for writing their names on the cardboard. After their rocks are dry, spray them with a clear acrylic spray to seal them and make them shinny. Then have them take their rocks home to use for paper weights or just for decoration. See example for size of rocks.

Recycle Art

Collect various clean containers such as margarine tubs, paper towel tubes, foil pie pans, empty pudding boxes, empty cereal boxes, packing peanuts, Popsicle sticks, berry baskets, buttons, pine cones, small sticks, small pebbles, dried weeds or flowers, empty lotion bottles and many other things you can think up. Also corn based packing foam sticks together when ends have been dampened.

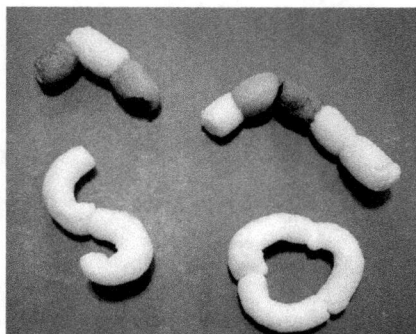

Place them on a table with scissors, glue, cardboard pieces, pencils, markers, paint and brushes. Tell the children that they can use the materials there and if they need something else to use for creating to ask you to find it for them. Tell them that they will be inviting another class and/or their parents to see their art exhibit when the pieces of art have been completed. When all the pieces have been completed, have your children help you set up and organize the items for the exhibit and make posters and invitations for it.

SENSORY

Put warm water with a small amount of dish soap for bubbles in the sensory table or pails. Then add water bottles, clean juice bottles and other plastic bottle in various sizes. Now add measuring pitchers and funnels. It is best to have children wear plastic aprons to protect them from the water.

Use a timer for taking turns if too many want to be there at the same time. Use a clip board and an attached pencil for children to sign their names if they want a turn. When it's their turn have them put a line through their name. Keep an eye on children to make sure that they are following the rules. Change the water each day and you can also change the color of the water by adding few drops of food coloring or bio color to the water.

Another fun thing to do is use pails with plant soil in them, put inside your sensory table. Put plant pots and artificial flowers with small shovels inside the table beside the pails of soil. Children will enjoy planting the flowers over and over again. You can get artificial flowers at the Dollar Store.

One more idea to help your children think of the earth and its beauty would be by placing plant /seed catalogs in the table with scissors. Children can cut out their favorite flowers and glue them to sheets of colored construction paper.

DRAMATIC PLAY & SOCIAL DEVELOPMENT

Set up a small tent or put up a card table with a small size sheet over it for a tent. Then add camping clothes such as red and black plaid shirts or camouflage shirts and hunting hats. You can often find them at a used clothing store. Now add dishes and pretend food, old cameras, binoculars, fishing poles with pretend fish to catch and stuffed animals. Add other items as you or the children think of them such as dolls and blankets. This will be a fun place for children to develop language skills and social skills. Keep a close eye on the tent with one end open at all times for safety of children.

Another idea would be to set up a vegetables and fruit stand with shelves for pretend fruits and vegetables. Have cash registers, pretend money with wallets and purses, balancing scales to weigh the produce, sacks for their produce and dress up clothing for moms, dads and children. Also don't forget to have dolls for the babies. You might set up small chairs for cars for the families to dive to the store.

SCIENCE

Set up the science table so that children can explore things that mix with water. Use items such as sand, dirt, salt and other things such as small pebbles. Using a spoon mix water with the ingredients in a small clear cups and see what happens. Then try other things mixed with the water. Did you guess what would happen? Did the water change the color? Which items were clear? Which were cloudy?

You can also sprout seeds such as alfalfa seed by placing them in a clear jar. Then place cheese cloth over the top of the bottle and fasten it closed with a strong elastic at the top of the bottle. Now put enough water into the jar to cover the seeds. Then turn the jar upside down to drain off water. Have the children help you put water in the jar and drain off the water three or more times a day. Soon children will see the seeds sprout. You can eat the sprouts on salad when they have grown. Store them in the fridge when they are the size you like to eat.

Another fun science experiment is done by cutting off the top of a carrot, beet and/or pineapple. Place crushed rocks or small pebbles in the bottom of a shallow container. Then add the tops and water to cover the bottom of container. Place where the container can get some light. Watch to see what happens next.

GROSS MOTOR SKILLS

Flower Throw

For this activity you will need to draw a large picture of a flower head and tape it in the center of the floor. Next you will need to use tape to mark around the circle places for the children to stand when throwing their bean bag. Put tape lines around the flower head about 3 feet back, then 5 feet back and 10 feet back from the center of the flower head.

Teacher will provide a bean or rice bag each of the children in this group activity.

Directions to make bean bag:

- Bags can be made by cutting two strong pieces of material such as cotton 5 inches by 5 inches.

- Then put the right sides of the pieces together.

- Place the sewing machine needle or regular needle if sewing by hand needle in the cloth ½ inch from the top edge.

- You will leave this edge open for now.

- Sew about ¼ inches from the edge on 3 sides of the cloth.

- Now turn the right sides out.

- Turn right side out and fill the bag about half full with the rice or beans.

- Next fold the top about ½ inch inside the bag.

- Pin the opening closed and sew across top two times to make it extra strong. See example steps.

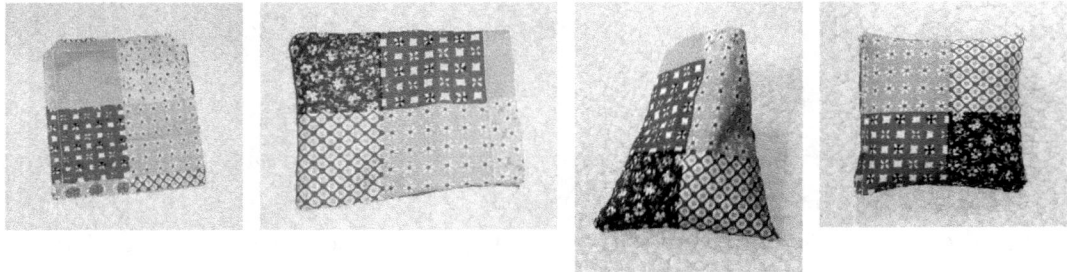

Now that the flower, lines, and the bean/rice bags are ready you can give the directions to the children.

Have the children in the group stand on the line closes to the flower. The teacher will instruct the children to throw their bean to the center of the flower when you say go. When you say get your bean bags children will pick up their bean bag. Remind them to look for their number or shape on the bag to get the correct one. Know children will stand on the line that is back farther than the last bag if they were able to throw the bag to land on the flower. If they didn't make it they will throw from the same place again upon your signal.

Children will continue as before – pick up their bags, notice if it is their bag and if it was on the flower. If it went on the flower, move back to the next line. Wait for the signal and throw again. Keep throwing until everyone has tried a number of times to hit the flower. Then save the items used and do it again another day. This activity will help them develop coordination and ability to aim and hit target.

Recycle Bowling

Save large pop bottles to make bowling pins fill the bottles with sand or water. Collect and fill 10 bottles and have a kick ball on hand. This game will be played outside. Play with a few children at a time, no more than four children. It is hard for them to wait for a turn.

Children will be about 5 feet from the pins and when that is too easy for them lengthen the distance. This game will be played like bowling with each child getting two turns to try and tip over all the pins by kicking the ball at them. Teacher will record how many pins each child knocked down. If they get all ten at one time they can bowl one more time. The game will last until each child has had five turns of two kicks each frame. Then you can total the points or just tell them that they all did a good job.

Obstacle Course

Set up a course outside in a circle design. Use tires to step in, cones to run around, hula hoop to twill around waist, tunnel (or large box) to crawl through, and a balance beam to walk on. The balance beam can be a 2x4 board. Tell them that they need to go carefully around the circle so they don't hurt others. Then show them how you want them to do it. Have students line up and go when you say to, so that they are not too close together doing the activity. Have them line back up when they have completed one turn and go again when you say. They really enjoy this activity and it helps them feel good about what they can do.

FIELD TRIP IDEAS

Arrange for the children to visit a recycling business if there is one near you. Get permission slips for each child and phone numbers and medical forms in case of problems. Also have parents come with you to help out. Plan for a snack to take with you and water for the children. Take a first aid kit as well. Have the children make individual thank you cards to take with you or make a poster size one and have all the children sign it.

Another place to go would be to a store that resells used clothing and household items. Ask if they will show the children how the store works and what they do to help people. Prepare for this trip the same way as going to the recycling business.

One more place to check out could be a garbage place where they recycle green waste by grinding up trees and branches and use it with leaves and lawn clipping to make mulch. People then can then buy the mulch to use the in their yard to keep weeds out and use less water for their yards. Talk with the children while they look at all the piles of garbage about how much room the garbage takes and how important it is to have less garbage. Prepare for this trip in the same manner as in the recycle tour.

Farm Animals & Dairy

🎵 MUSIC AND MOVEMENT

"Flick a Fly" from Walter The Waltzing Worm by Hap Palmer, Educational Activities, INC. This fun song has children flicking a fly from various parts of their body.

"Walter the Waltzing Worm: from Walter the Waltzing Worm," Educational Activities, INC. Children use a small piece of rope to be a worm and the song tells children the movement to do with the worm. Example swing, shake, twist and stretch.

"Make Friends With a Bean Bag" from Bean Bag Activities & Coordination Skills. This tape is full of fun ways for children to gain coordination skills.

"Five Little Ducklings" from Finger Plays, The Story Teller Inc. The company offers felt figures for gloves and felt figures for flannel stories.

"Fuzzy Little Bunnies" from Finger Plays, The Story Teller Inc.

"Down on Grandpa's Farm" from Barney's Favorites volume 1, Columbia House. This is a fun song where the children join in to make the sounds of the farm animals.

"Six Little Ducks" from Barney's Favorites volume 1, Columbia House. This song has children interact by holding in their fingers to the number of duck and voices to quack.

"Bingo" from Barney's Favorites volume 1, Columbia House. This song is easy for children to learn with lots of repetition and fun clapping for missing letters in the farm dogs name – Bingo. This also learn the letter names in his name.

"Baa Baa Black Sheep" from Singable Songs for the Very Young by Raffi part 1, Manufactured and distributed by Rounder Records. This song is fun and can be changed by changing the colors, the people and or the animals.

"Old MacDonald Had A Band" from Singable Songs for the Very Young by Raffi part 1, Manufactured and distributed by Rounder Records. This is a fun song that gets the children pretending to play the various instruments and making their sounds.

"Listen to the Horses" from More Singable Songs by Raffi.

"Grandma's Farm" from Witches' Brew by Hap Palmer, Educational Activities Inc. This is a simple song that helps teach the animal sounds.

"The Farmer in the Dell" from Wee Sing Grandpa's Magical Toys, Price Stern Sloon, Inc. This tape has children singing and holding hands while going around in a circle. Pick a farmer to be in the center and during the appropriate time that child will pick a wife/husband and etc.

"Harry the Horse" from Making Music with Mother Goose, Pocket Productions, www.csag.com/fingerplays CD by Jane Kitson.

"Who Lives in the Big Red Barn?" from Making Music with Mother Goose, Pocket Productions, www.csag.com/fingerplays CD by Jane Kitson.

"Cock A Doddle Do!" from Making Music with Mother Goose, Pocket Productions, www.csag.com/fingerplays CD by Jane Kitson.

"Fox in the Hen House" from Making Music with Mother Goose, Pocket Productions, www.csag.com/fingerplays CD by Jane Kitson.

"Barnyard Song" from Really Silly Songs! Wonder Workshop, Inc. This is a fun song to sing along with and make the various sounds of farm animals.

"The Old Gray Mare" from Really Silly Songs! Wonder Workshop, Inc.

"Turkey In The Straw" from Really Silly Songs! Wonder Workshop, Inc.

"If You Were a Farmer" from My Toes Are Starting To Wiggle! by "Miss Jackie" Silberg. This book includes sheet music, words and activities to do with the songs and a tape is also available for all the songs.

"Six Big Cows" from My Toes Are Starting To Wiggle! by "Miss Jackie" Silberg.

"The Little Mice" from My Toes Are Starting To Wiggle! by "Miss Jackie" Silberg.

The Farmer in the Dell" from My Toes Are Starting To Wiggle! by "Miss Jackie" Silberg.

"Six Little Ducks That Once Knew" from <u>My Toes Are Starting To Wiggle!</u> by "Miss Jackie" Silberg.

"Yippee, Yippee, Yee" from "Macmillian Sing & Learn Program by Newbridge Communications, Inc. This song has children dancing to a caller and shouting yipee! It's lots of fun.

"Rabbit Dance" from Macmillian Sing & Learn Program by Newbridge Communications, Inc. Children will have lots of fun hopping with this song.

"Duck Waddle" from Macmillian Sing & Learn Program by Newbridge Communications, Inc. Everyone will be waddling with this song.

"The Barnyard" from Macmillian Sing & Learn Program by Newbridge Communications, Inc. Children will be busy making farm animal sounds with this song.

"Egg to Chick" from Macmillian Sing & Learn Program by Newbridge Communications, Inc. Children will act out the growing of a chick with this song.

"Noisy House" from Macmillian Sing &Learn Program by Newbridge Communications, Inc. This tape is a story with children taking part as a chorus of animal sounds.

"The Three Little Pigs" from Macmillian Sing & Learn Program by Newbridge Communications, Inc. This is a story tape that children act out the parts with the tape.

"Color Hoedown" from Macmillian Sing & Learn Program by Newbridge Communications, Inc. This is one of my favorite songs because it is fun for the children to dance to and helps them listen to color names and do the actions of each color word.

Songs are a fun way for children to develop language, thinking, creativity, self-worth and large/small muscles. The simple songs are usually best to start learning. They give children confidence that they can sing and it makes them happy.

Adding action songs such as "The Farmer in the Dell" helps them enjoy the music through movement so they are not having to just sit still while learning. Another idea is to use pictures when teaching new songs to remind them of the words in the song. Repeating new songs often will help their self-confidence grow and they will learn to enjoy music.

LANGUAGE AND LITERACY

Five Little Ducks by Pamela Paparone, Scholastic, Inc.

Webster J. Duck by Martin Waddell, illustrated by David Parkins, Scholastic, Inc.

Daisy and the Monster by Jane Simmons, Scholastic, Inc.

Inside a Barn in the Country by Alyssa Satin Capucilli, illustrated by Tedd Arnold, Scholastic, Inc.

Over in the Meadow by Paul Galdone, Simon and Schuster Books for Young Readers.

No Milk by Jennifer A. Ericsson with pictures by Ora Eitan, Tambourine Books.

Duck on a Bike by David Shannon, Scholastic, Inc.

Horses and Ponies by E. M. McGowan, KIDSBOOKS, Inc.

Wake Up, Wake Up! by Brian and Rebecca Wildsmith, Scholastic, Inc.

The Little Red Hen by Paul Galdone, Clarion Books a Houghton Miffin Company Imprint.

Chickens Aren't the Only Ones by Ruth Heller, Scholastic, Inc.

Over on the Farm: A Counting Picture Book Rhyme by Christopher Gunson, Scholastic, Inc.

Oink! Moo! How Do You Do? by Grace Maccarone, illustrated by Hans Wilhem, Scholastic, Inc.

There's a Cow in the Road! by Reeve Lindbergh, pictures by Tracey Campbell Pearson, Dial Books for Young Readers, a division of Penguin Books USA.

Have You Got My Purr? by Judy West, illustrated by Tim Warners, Scholastic, Inc.

Hopper by Marcus Pfister, Scholastic, Inc.

Seven Blind Mice by Ed Young, Scholastic, Inc.

The Three Little Pigs by Shogo Hirata, Modern Publishing.

The Three Billy Goats Gruff by Stephen Carpenter, Scholastic, Inc.

The Day the Goose Got Loose by Reeve Lindbergh, Pictures by Steven Kellogg, Scholastic, Inc.

To Market To Market by Anne Miranda, illustrated by Janet Stevens, Scholastic, Inc.

Farmer Brown Goes Round and Round by Teri Sloat, illustrated by Nadine Bernard Westcott, Scholastic, Inc.

Who Took The Farmer's Hat? by Joan L. Nodset, Pictures by Fritz Siebel Scholastic, Inc.

Farm Flu by Teresa Bateman, illustrated by Nadine Bernard Westcott, Scholastic, Inc.

The Tale of Peter Rabbit by Beatrix Potter, Golden Press Western Publishing Company, Inc.

Pancakes For Breakfast by Tomie DePaola, Scholastic, Inc.

The Grumpy Morning by Pamela Duncan Edwards, illustrated by Darcia Labrosse, Scholastic, Inc.

I'm Going To Be A Farmer by Edith Kunhardt, Scholastic, Inc.

Circle Helps

Use songs that are simple and fun to gather the children over to the circle. Choose ones with your theme in mind and if they can clap or move to them it works even better to get them involved.

Read the books and become acquainted with them before reading to the children. If the book has more words to each page than can hold your children's interest, try telling that part of story in your own words by simplifying it.

Ask parents from your class if they have lived or worked on a dairy farm and would like to share information about it with the children. Be sure and ask them ahead of time, so that they can be prepared and also ask them to tell it in a simple way. Also give them a time limit so it won't be too long for the children. If they can bring any pictures or equipment, that would help the children understand the subject better. Be sure and thank them and have the children make them thank you cards.

You can also get them involved by having them make butter at the circle. Buy liquid cream at the grocery store and buy small clear plastic tubs with lids at the dollar store. Also bring clean marbles. Leave the cream out of the fridge long enough to take the chill off so it will set up faster.

Tell the children that they will make butter today using cream from cows. Pour a little of the cream into each container and add a marble. Then put the lid on securely. Now tell the children to carefully shake the container while you sing a few songs. Stop after each song and have them look through the clear plastic to see if it looks solid like butter. The marble helps it to mix up. When there is a small ball inside with milk around it, stop open the container and place the ball of butter in a dish and pour off the buttermilk into a pitcher.

When all of the butter has been made, have soda crackers ready at the table to spread the butter on and small bathroom cups for children to try a small taste of the butter milk. As you dismiss them from the circle have them wash their hands and set at the table. A helper should be at the table to help with the butter and buttermilk. While at the table ask children open ended questions about the activity. Such as, "What did you do to get butter? "or "What happened to the cream?"

SMALL GROUP ACTIVITIES/TABLE TIMES

MATH & COGNITIVE

Apples on the Tree

Use construction paper to make a tree with a brown trunk and green to represent the leaves. Then color copy it ten times. Next add one number from 1-10 on each tree and cover it with clear contact paper or laminate them. That way they can be cleaned and used many times. Now buy red foam sheets and punch out or cut out 60 small apples. This will give you five extra apples for when they drop or lose a few. See example of tree.

To play the game, pass out one card to each of the children in your small group. Have them look at the number on their card and then take apples from a pile. They will count the apples one at a time while placing them on their tree. When child reaches the number on their card they will stop adding apples.

Now have the children take turns counting the apples on their tree to you to check for accuracy.

Next give each child a new card and have them proceed as before. Continue counting and exchanging cards until you see that they are starting to be less interested. If the children need help identifying the numbers on their card, hold up that many fingers. Then have them count your fingers to discover the number on their card. Now count with them until they reach the number on their card.

Cow Bingo

Draw or trace an outline of a cow and then draw squares into of the drawing. Then copy the picture five times, so that each of the children in your small group will be able to have a card. Now write numbers inside the squares from 1-10. Place the numbers in different places on each card. This is done so that the children will not be able to just look as their neighbor's card to place a marker. Next cover the cards with clear contact paper or laminate them. See example of cow.

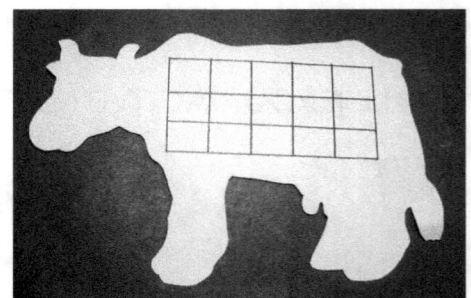

Now make a calling number list of the numbers 1-10 on card-stock and also make squares with each number on one. Provide beans for markers or you can use eatable markers for the children to eat when the game time is over such as fruit loop cereal, animal crackers, fruit snack or other small items.

To play the game teacher will hold up one of the number squares for them to see and say the number. Children will look on their card for that number and if they have it they will place a marker on it. Play will continue until one of the children's cards is covered with markers. Then the child will say BINGO! That child will then say each of the numbers that he/she has markers on.

Other children will check their cards to see if they missed covering one of their numbers. If the child that said BINGO has all the numbers that have been called on his/her card, he/she can eat their treat markers and/or leave the group. The rest of the children will leave their markers on their card. The game will continue as before, until all of the children have had a turn with filling their bingo card. Then they will also be been able to eat their treat.

Match the Shape

Make a shape card for each of the children in the small group to use. The shapes will include each of the following: square, circle, triangle and rectangle on each card in a different order. The teacher will also make a copy of each shape on the card and make enough shapes for each child's card.

The children will take turns picking up a shape, saying its name and matching it to that shape on their card. Play continues until all of the shapes have been identified. Then you can change cards and play the game again.

Harder Shape Game

Draw pictures using shapes such as circles, squares, rectangles, triangles, diamonds, ovals, hearts, stars, octagons and or crescents. Make copies of the shapes used in the pictures. Then the teacher will laminate or cover them with clear contact paper. See example of card.

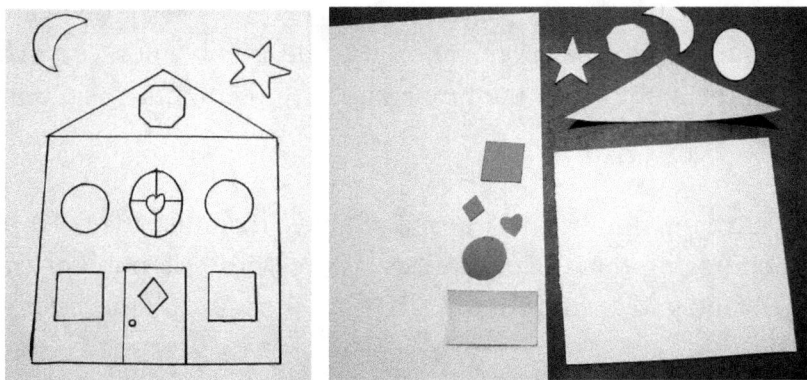

Children will each be given a picture card and matches to the shapes on their card. The children will take turns placing a matched shape to their card and saying the shapes name. Play continues until the cards have all the matching shapes on them. Now if the group wants to they can trade cards and shape pieces to play the game again.

Match the Coins

Make a card for each of the children in her/his small group by taping coins on one side of the card and leaving a column next to them to place the matching coins. Use the coins penny, nickel, dime and quarter.

This small group is for children that need more of a challenge and can count to 25. Teacher will have a roll of pennies available for use of children. Have the child look at one penny and place it next to the penny on the card. Next have the child place one penny at a time in a line and count up to five. Have the child look at the nickel on the number card and tell him/her that the five pennies represent the nickel. Have the child place a nickel next to the matching coin and have them say a nickel is like having five pennies.

Proceed in the same way with the dime and then the quarter. Another day have them show you how many pennies makes a nickel, dime and a quarter. Review with them the way you did it the first day. Asking how many pennies represent the nickel, dime and quarter. Also have them march the coins and say their names. Keep working on this a little each week so that they understand it better each week.

Match the Amounts

Make set of cards for each child in your small group of the numbers 1-10. Start out by using cards 1-5 and later adding 6-10 when they have learned the amount each of the numbers 1-5 represent. Use tokens such as Lima beans or Cheerios cereal for counting. Teacher will place number card sets by each child along with some of the tokens.

Then tell children to choose a number card and place that many tokens by the card that shows the amount that the number represents. When they have one card completed, have them call you over so that they can count the number for you. Then they can continue to match the amounts to the numerals. Give them lots of encouragement and help if needed.

Later when they have the numbers 1-5 mastered, have them use the 6-10 cards with the tokens. Keep encouraging them. Continue as before with one number card at a time. When they understand and are able to do 6-10 have them use all the cards and put them in order from 1-10.

FINE MOTOR SKILLS

Pig Pen

Draw a three sided pen with the back side line thick and the other two lines thin. Then draw at the end open end, a medium sized dot on each of thin lines. See example of pen. Then copy this sheet enough times for all the children in the class, but they will do the sheet in small groups. Provide pencils for children and a ruler for each child.

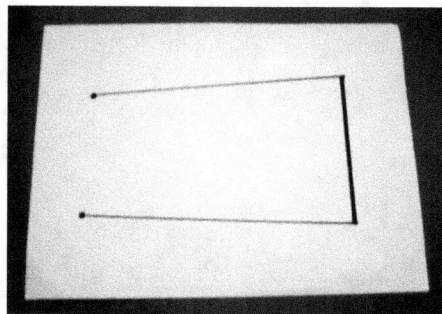

For this activity children will write their name on the back of their paper. Then turn the paper over and make a line from the top of the thick line to the bottom of it by keeping their pencil line on the thick line as much as they can. Next they will use a ruler and line up the ruler on the two dots. Hold ruler with one hand and press the pencil against the edge of the ruler while making a line from one dot to the next dot. This will close the pen and give them an idea of how to use a ruler.

Now children will draw pigs or other farm animals inside the pen. This activity will help them practice using a pencil and a ruler while making a drawing of animals.

Mud on the Farm

Provide heavy pieces of white poster board that has been divided and cut into four equal pieces. Cut and prepare a piece for each child in the class. Teacher will also supply instant chocolate pudding that has been made with water and has been chilled in the fridge until time to use it.

Children will wear an apron to protect their clothing. Give each child in the small group a piece of the poster board and a scoop of chocolate pudding. Children will use their fingers to move the pudding (mud) all over their paper to make a mud picture. They can also if they would like before they start their mud picture, draw and cut out an animal to put in their mud picture.

They will press their picture into the mud after spreading the mud around. Hang pictures to dry on a drying rack or on a clothes line that is over a protected area to keep it off the floor. It could be outside or inside over paper or a plastic shower curtain. Have a pail with warm sudsy water ready for them to wash off most of the pudding before going to the sink to get the rest washed off, saves mess on the floor and walls while they travel to the sink.

Ice Cream Cones

Make patterns on heavy paper for children to trace of cones and scoops. Then allow children to pick the colors of paper to trace their cone and scoops of ice cream on to. Now they are ready to cut out their patterns and glue their cone together. Example of scoops and cone shown.

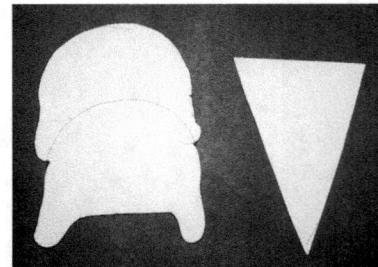

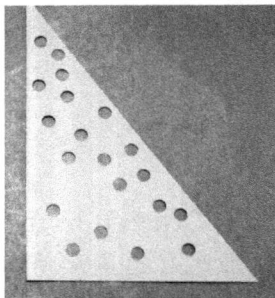

Swiss Cheese

Teacher will use a paper cutter to cut triangle pieces of yellow and orange paper. Provide the children with paper punches and have them punch many holes in their paper to create Swiss cheese. This activity helps develop hand and finger strength. See example of Swiss cheese.

Duck, Rabbit or Fish

This unique shape shown in the example can be either a duck, rabbit or a fish. Show the children the different ways to hold their paper to make the three different animals. Have them decide which animal or animals they want to make and choose a color of paper that would make that animal look the way that they want it to look. Make the shape patterns for children to trace around. Then provide paper in different colors for them to trace the pattern on so they can make one or more different animals.

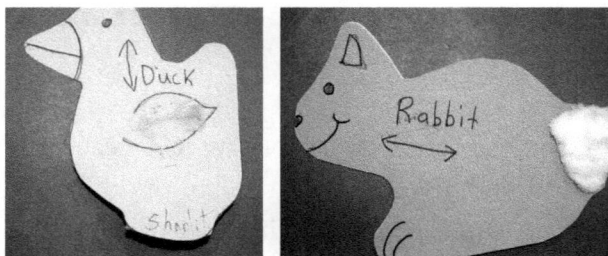

Now have scissors available to cut out their tracing of one or more animals. Next have them turn their paper to make the desired animal and provide markers to draw in the animal's features. Also provide glue so that they can add feathers for a birds, cotton balls for rabbits or even noodles for scales on the fish. This activity will have children having fun while developing their cutting, drawing, tracing and gluing skills.

Cow Milking

Make one or more pretend cows for children to milk. Obtain a box/boxes for the cow. The top of the box will become the bottom of the cow by cutting it with and upward curve on all sides. This will form the legs. See example of box. Then use poster paint to paint the cow white with black spots. Next use poster board to draw the cows head and cut in out. Then mount it to one end of the box. Now use a piece of braided rope for the tail and tape it to the opposite end of the head. If don't have rope just draw a tail and tape it to the cow.

This next part is important for milking. You will need a rubber glove for the children to milk. You can fill glove with water or use a little white paint in the water to make it look like milk. Then you must tie the end closed so water stays in glove. Next make a small hole in the middle of the box. This is where you will push the end knot through to the top of the cows body. To make the knot more secure have a small clear lip and cut a small cross shape in the middle and push the knot through it like you did for the box and tape it with strong tape.

When the cow box is completed place a small bowl or pail under the cow's udder to catch the milk. You will need to use a large diaper pin or a large needle to pierce each of the fingers, so that the milk will come out when gently pulled on. Children really enjoy this fine motor activity. Have other bags of milk in reserve for when that bag is empty. Another way to use this on a different day is to add brown to color it or other colors and let them squirt it onto paper to create a picture.

Sponge Paint Farm Animal

Make the outline of a animal such as a pig, cow, horse or etc. Then cut picture out and make several copies for children to trace around. You can have them cut them out or just leave the animal tracing on their paper to sponge paint. Before they paint, have them wear aprons to keep clean and write their names on the back of their paper.

Have several colors of poster paint set out. The paint should be mixed with a little liquid dish soap to help the paint wash off. Use flat containers for the paint mixture and thin the paint a little with water so it's not too thick. A large sponge can be cut into smaller pieces for children use. You may want to attach a clothes pin to one end of the sponge. In this manner children can hold on to the end not in the paint, while dipping the other end into the paint. The sponge should then be pressed in an up and down motion. by moving the sponge from the paint to the paper it will cause a design print on the animal.

Play Dough Animals

Make play dough for children using the recipe below. Children will be encouraged to make animals from the dough. You can use the type of dough that will dry out so that they can paint it or the soft pliable type that is easy to reform.

<u>Self-Hardening Play Dough</u>

4 cups flour	1 1/2 cups salt
1 tsp alum	3/4-1 1/2 cups water
*Optional 1-2 Tbs. Food coloring	

Mix the flour, salt and alum together. Then add the water to it gradually. *If you want mixture colored, add coloring to water before stirring it into the flour. This helps the color to be consistent and smooth.

Stir to form a ball in bowl. Add more water if it won't hold together. Next knead the dough. Place in a sealed container or bag until ready to use. After shapes have been made leave them out to dry or put in oven at a low temperature for a few minutes. Then turn off the oven and keep the door shut to help the dough dry out quicker without cooking it.

<u>Soft Pliable Baby Oil Play Dough</u>

2 cups flour	1 cup salt
2 Tbl. Cream of tartar	2 cups water
1 1/2-2 Tbl Baby Oil	*Optional food color

*If you are using food coloring add it first to the water before adding it with other ingredients. Mix ingredients together in a pan. Cook over medium heat until stiff and dough falls away from the sides of the pan. Turn out onto a counter top, let cool and then knead. Knead for a few minutes. Place in sealed container or bag.

Black or White Sheep

Teacher will make an outline of a sheep and copy it onto heavy paper a few times, so that children can trace around it and cut it out on black or white paper. If you don't want them to cut it out have a parent cut them out for you as a volunteer. Then have small glue bottles and cotton balls for the children to stretch out and glue to their sheep. See example of sheep.

LANGUAGE AND LITERACY

Writing and Reading With Children

Children in a small group will look at the wordless pictures book titled <u>Pancakes For Breakfast</u> by Tomie De Paola. Then we will look at the pictures once again and take turns having the child make words for the picture by asking questions like, "What do you thinking is happening?" "How do you know that?" and "Why did they do that?" Teacher will write on sticky notes what the child says and place the note on that page with child's name. Continue doing this until each child has at least two turns. Now read the book using their words.

Sorting Pictures

Acquire pictures of farm equipment, foods grown at farms and dairy products. Use magazines that are found in pet stores, seed catalogs, food magazines and farming equipment catalogs to get the pictures needed. Then mount the pictures and laminate them.

Have children in small groups come to the table and ask them to put the pictures that go together into three different groups. Have them do this by taking turns picking pictures. Have each child express how or why they go together. Continue until they have categorized all the pictures. Next have an another group come to take a turn and proceed as before.

Ice Cream

Have a small group of children come to your table to learn how to make ice cream and to make a small individual amount for them to eat. Talk about the importance of measuring the ingredients and following the directions in the recipe. Have children help you as much as possible. I will give directions for two ways you can make ice cream.

Number 10 Can Method

You will need: clean #10 can with a plastic lid that seals and a smaller container about a 3 pound can or a rubber type one that seals and fits inside the larger one. You will also need to decide how many batches you will make and double the amounts accordingly.

One Batch

1 egg	½ cup sugar
1 cup of milk	1 cup of whipping cream
1 teaspoon vanilla	rock salt
crushed ice	

Have the children take turns putting the ingredients into the small container and then put the lid on and seal it closed with duct tape. Place it inside the large can and have the children place some crushed ice around the small can and then add rock salt around small can. Then add more crushed ice around container and a layer of rock salt. Continue layering ice with salt until container is full. Next put the lid on the large can and tape it with duct tape. Now have the children sit on the floor and roll the can back and worth to each other. Have them notice that frost forms on the outside of the large can. Continue rolling the can for about 10 minutes.

Then open the outer can and remove the smaller one with the ingredients. Next remove the lid and stir up the ingredients and scrape the sides with a spatula. Now replace the lid. Drain off the ice water from the lager can and put smaller container back in large can and pack it with ice and salt. Seal container again and then roll back and forth for five more minutes. Take off the lids. It is now ready to eat and enjoy. It makes about 3 cups.

I have taken the prepared the ice cream containers on walks with the children. When we reached the desired location, we sat on the grass and rolled the can. It was great fun to make the ice cream there and eat it on warm days. It turned out great. If you have a large group, prepare two cans to take with you. I also took these items with the can: small bathroom cups and plastic spoons, hand wipes and a garbage bag.

Second Way Ice Cream

I used the same recipe, but I used a bowl to mix the ingredients. Then I used lunch size plastic seal bags to put the ice and salt layers in with snack size bags to put the ingredients. Tape the small bags and large bags in addition to sealing them. Then have the children carefully shake and roll the bags back and forth. The clear bags enable you to see when the ice cream has set up, so you know when to help the children open them to eat from their own bag with a spoon. This is a good way for each to have a small taste of ice cream for each child and they get to make their own.

These two methods help children participate together to develop social skills, thinking processes, numbers and following directions.

Sequencing Chick

Draw an egg, an egg with a small crack, an egg with a large crack with a little of a chick peaking through the crack, an egg with the shell open and displaying the chick and last a picture with the shell open all the play and a view of the chick. After making these simple drawings print enough of them for each child in your class plus one copy for a master.

Next cut an oval around each shape and sort them into small plastic bags, so that each child will have a full set. You can cut strips of construction paper for children to glue their egg to chick on in correct sequential order or just have them practice ordering them on the table. Check with each child as they try to arrange them and ask them which comes first and which comes last. Also have them tell you why the one they have choose should be the next one by describing the reason. See the example.

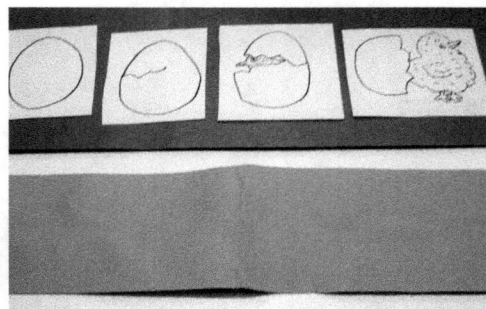

Little Red Hen

Read or tell the story of the Little Red Hen using pictures from the book or picture sticks. You can make picture sticks by coping pictures of the main characters in the book and mount them on craft sticks. Next have the children take turns retelling parts of the story using pictures or picture sticks. This will help children increase their expressive language skills and thinking skills.

Make a Book

Read to a small group the book Farm Flu by Teresa Bateman or another book and have the children take turns telling you what their favorite animal was from the book and why he/she liked it. Then have them use paper, pencil and crayons to make a picture to put in a class book. Have them tell you about their picture and write their words for the page. Use a loose-leaf journal to place each child's picture in to form their own book. Be sure and include their name with their picture. Place the completed book in the children library so that they can read and look at it.

Match the Baby Animals

Check out books about farm animals and obtain pictures of adult animals as well as their young. Copy a picture of the adult animal and another one of the baby animal. Write down the names for each such at cat-adult & kitten-baby, dog-adult & puppy baby, cow-adult & calf-baby, chicken-adult & chick-baby, goat-adult & kid-baby, pig-adult & piglet-baby, duck-adult & duckling baby. Mount your pictures so they can be used again.

Have your small group come to the table and show one picture at a time to them. Have them take turns telling you what animal it is, what sound it makes, what it eats, what the adult or mom/dad is called and what the baby is called. Go through all your cards. When you have talked about and shown each animal, go back through the cards and ask the names for the adult and the baby animal.

FREE TIME

CREATIVE ARTS

Plate Painting

Mix food coloring with small amounts of canned sweetened condensed milk in small bowl. Set the bowl on the table with small watercolor brushes and/or droppers with paper plates. Encourage children to paint on them. Have them place art on a flat surface to dry. When they are dry, they have pretty gloss shine to them. Hang them around the room or let them take them home. See example.

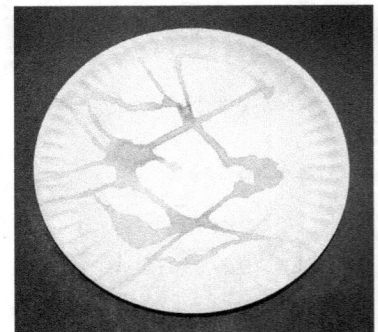

Collage

Set out pieces of cardboard with glue, scissors, construction paper, different colors of yarn and small pieces of cloth. Let the child design, cut and glue on their cardboard pieces.

Watercolor

Set out large and small pieces of watercolor paper with small and medium sized brushes. Tell them to paint whatever they would like on the paper.

SENSORY

Put sand or wheat in sensory table or in dish pails. Then provide small farm animals with craft sticks (for fences), berry baskets (for cages), also provide little people for children to interact with the animals and/or other children.

Another idea to use is to put warm water into the sensory table or dish pails. Then put in floating ducks with numbers written on the bottoms of them. You could also provide a net to catch them with a pail to put the ducks in while they putting them in numeral order.

You could also put floating fish with paper clips attached and alphabet letters written on them. Provide fishing poles with strong magnet on the end of their lines. Have floating plastic containers to place the caught fish.

DRAMATIC PLAY & SOCIAL DEVELOPMENT

Build a farmyard in the dramatic play center including a sawhorse cow with a fence and a painted barn. Starting with a sawhorse, some cut boards and a large refrigerator box, have the children help to brainstorm ways to construct these structures to create a farmyard. Give children opportunities to see how various kinds of dairy products are made by making butter and ice cream.

With the children's ideas and a variety of materials available, make the barnyard scene, adding new parts to it each day. Ask children questions such as, "What should we add to make it look more like a farm?" "How should we nail these boards together so that they will stand up like a fence?"

Also provide props that will encourage them to pretend to be farmers and farm animals. They might have Halloween costumes of farm animals they could bring and/or cowboy/cowgirl thing they could bring to wear.

Use your block area as part of your dramatic area by providing large farm animals close to the blocks. Children can make pens for the animals and fences. You can also encourage the children to make and tape signs that tell others what kinds of animals live in the different sized pens and other information like, keep gate closed so horses don't get out.

You could extend your classroom to include your outside sand area. Use child size rakes, hoes and shovels to plant real potatoes and/or carrots. The children in our class loves digging holes for the potatoes and carrots and later digging them back up again.

Additionally, you could provide stick horses outside for the children to ride on. You can use a thick dowel stick with a picture of a horse head attached onto one end, just put the dowel between the right and left side head picture.

SCIENCE

Place a shallow dish on the table with wheat on top of a wet sponge. Keep the sponge wet and watch it grow. Later you can add the sprouted wheat to a green salad and have them taste it. Also provide pea or bean seeds. These seeds are cheap and easy to grow. They also are big and will have larger roots for the children to see. Have them place them into a small Ziploc bag with two wet cotton balls inside. Then tape them onto a window to watch them grow. You can also provide a frame out of constriction paper to place their bags. Example is shown.

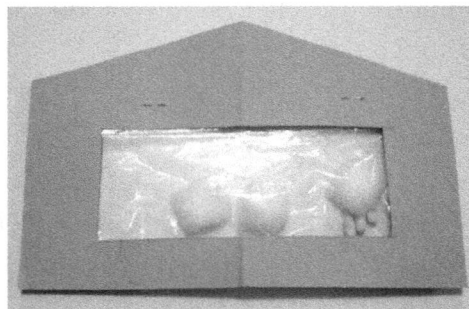

Also provide various packages of vegetable seeds for the children to examine. Keep a magnifying glass on the table for them to look at the sprouting wheat and seeds.

Don't forget to include farm and farm animal books for them to look at and ask others to read to them about things that they are interested.

GROSS MOTOR SKILLS

Duck, Duck, Goose

If the weather is nice, play some fun running games such as Duck, Duck Goose. In this game the children stand or sit in a circle with one child walking around the outside of the circle touching each child lightly on the shoulder and saying "Duck" or "Goose." If the child says "Duck" nothing happens and the child continues walking around the circle.

But if the child says "Goose" and touches a child's shoulder the child who has been touched runs after the child that touched him/her and tries to touch him/her. The child that did the touching runs in the same direction as he/she was when walking around the circle. He/she tries to get back to the place that he/she touched the child.

At the same time the child, that got touched is trying to catch up with the child that touched him or her and touch him/her. If the child is successful in touching the child before the child arrives back to where the touching occurred he/she can sit back down. But if the child chasing doesn't get the child running from him/her in time, that person is now "it." The game continues as before with new child choosing someone to touch and say goose.

Parachute Play

Have children stand around a large parachute ad hold on to a handle. Tell the children that it is important to listen and follow the directions that you give so that it will be a fun experience. Ask what might happen if only part of the children held the parachute up when it was time to raise them. Now ask them to all raise their arms up while holding the parachute. Now have them pull their hands holding the chute down.

Then have the children raise and lower the chute quickly. Say see how fun it is when we all work together. Do this a few times and then have them place the chute down and place stuffed farm animals in the middle of the chute. Tell the children to raise the chute if the animals on their side and close to the edge and might fall off and put the chute down if not. Have fun lifting and lowering the chute and watching what happens to the animals. Pick the animals up that fall out and toss them onto the chute again. Before they get tired of the activity stop and then do it another day.

Bean Bag Toss

Before doing this activity have bean or rice bags ready to use and make a target. Use a large piece of cardboard to draw a picture on then paint it with poster paint. The picture can be an animal or just a circle target with a bulls eye in the center. Have a few children at a time use the bean bags to try and hit the target, so the line isn't long. The other children can be using basketballs to throw and catch with partners.

Pillow Case Race

Teacher will provide children with a pillow case. Get old ones from parents or go to used clothing stores to purchase some. Make a starting line with masking tape at one end of grass and a finish line at the other end. Tell children to put their feet and legs into the pillow case and hold it with their hands on each side as they hop to the finish line. Have part of the children sitting or standing on the side lines to cheer them on until it is their turn. Then have others race and cheer for them.

Throw the Cube

Make a large cube by covering a square box size 4 inches by 4 inches with stick pictures of children doing various activities such as jumping jacks, toe touching, spinning around on their bottom, running in place and hopping on one foot.

Children will take turns rolling the large die and then all the children will do the movement picture that landed face up on the floor. Each child will have two turns. Example is shown.

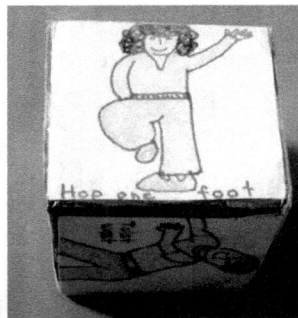

Spoon Egg Balance

Children will be placed into teams of no more than five people each so they will not be standing around a lot of the time waiting for their turn. Teacher will tape a line for starting and a line to across before turning to go back to the starting line. Teacher will give the first child in each team a large table spoon with a plastic egg to put in it.

On the signal, the first person in each line will place the egg in their spoon and carefully walk to the turning line and then walk back to the starting line while holding the egg carefully. If the egg drops, the child will stop and pick it up and continue on. When the child has gone to the starting place she/he will give the spoon and egg to first person in their line and then go to the back of their line. The new front person will take the spoon and put egg in spoon and proceed as the first child did. Play continues in this manner until everyone has had a turn.

FIELD TRIP IDEAS

Teacher will ask parents in a note if they know of a good place for the children to see farm animals. This may help you find a destination for the field trip. Also check with other teachers for a good place to go. You can also check the internet and/or phone book.

In my area, there is a commercial farm place to go for a small fee. The children can see farm animals and pet most of them. They also give the children a ride on a hay wagon. If you can't find a place where they have lots of animals, try going to several different place to see horses, cows, chickens and /or ducks. Try to go in the spring when the animals are having babies. You might also go to a park that has a pond with ducks and fish.

If you live in an area without any of these types of things, see if you can go to a dairy farm or milk processing plant where milk and their products are prepared and distributed.

Be sure and take emergency forms, first aid kit, thank you notes, camera and small snacks with water. Have parents go with you for extra help.

Extra

Birthdays

Every child likes to celebrate their birthday, but some birthdays are when children aren't in school and they may be left out. This is what I do to make sure they aren't left out. At the first of the year and whenever a new child starts school I find out when their birthday is and write it on a birthday poster with all the children's birthdays on it. Then if their birthday will fall on a weekend or holiday, I find a date that the parent and child would like to celebrate it, so that it is close to that date and we are in school.

Before that day I have the parent with their child take home a poster. The poster has places for them to record information. I give the parent a list with suggestions to put on the poster. The following is a list of items on the note:

- What is your favorite color?

- Please draw or include a photo of your family.

- When is your birthday?

- How old are you now?

- Do you have a pet?

- What pet would you have if you did have one?

- Tell us more about the pet you have or would like.

- Draw or show a photo of pet you have or would like pet.

- What food do like for dinner?

- What is your favorite dessert?

The child brings back the completed poster and tells about it at circle time on their special day. This information will help the other children know the child better and can help the child to feel special. Then put the poster on the wall for the rest of the day and then return it to their parent.

They can also bring a special toy or book that they would like to show us. Next we all sing a song called "Special Me" by Dr. Jean from CD "Ole! Ole! Ole!" (The songs on the CD are great for routine songs, learning songs, just for fun songs and ending songs. It also is great because each song is in English and Spanish.)

If the child's birthday is in the summer or during along Christmas break, I schedule a half year birthday with the parents. The child's poster is used as mentioned before and so is the special time at the circle with that child. During each child's special day we have a birthday crown for the child to wear and I take their picture wearing it. See example of crown. They also get to be the leader in going outside and going to activities after circle time.

Un-Birthdays

Having an un-birthday can be a fun activity to have on a cold wintery day or any time when a just for fun day is needed. In the original movie of Alice in Wonderland they sang, "A Very Merry Un-birthday to You." I like to explain to the children that today is nobody's birthday in our class, so we are all going to have a very merry un-birthday.

We will <u>sing</u> "A Very Merry Un-birthday to Us." We will play pin the nose on the clown. Teacher will draw simple face on a poster board and leave off the nose. Make colorful round noses for each child to pin their nose on the clown. Children will <u>take turns</u> closing their eyes tight and walk forward with their nose to try and place it on the clown without peeking. Wherever they touch first is where the teacher will tape it. Then the other children will take turns. Used this activity for fun social interactions.

Next we will play musical chairs. We play it for <u>fun exercise</u> without the hurt feelings of not winning. They all win because instead of taking a chair out each time a child can't find one to sit on when the music stops we don't take one out. Instead each child finds a chair that they were not setting on last time the music stopped. Use music recordings children like while doing this activity.

For a <u>fine motor activity</u>, have construction paper crown laid out with various items for the children to glue on their crown, such as small buttons, sequins, small pom poms, yarn, colored noodles and feathers. When the crowns are dry, staple them into circles for children to take home.

For a <u>cognitive</u> activity, the teacher will cut out from magazines a picture of a baby, a child crawling, a small child walking and a child riding a tricycle. Then mount them onto papers and make copies of them. Each child in your small group should have their own set to use at the table. Laminate them so that they will last and you can reuse them.

When the children come to the table remind them that they used to be babies, but now you go to school. Have them talk about what babies do and what they can't do yet. Then talk about older children and what they can do. Then pass out the sets of the pictures and ask them to place them in order of youngest to oldest. When they have arranged them one at a time have them tell you why they placed the pictures the way they did. After the child is through have them go to another activity.

For a <u>math and fine motor activity</u>, teacher will draw a large cake on card stock and copy one for each child to use. Teacher will also mix shaving cream with white craft glue and food coloring. It only takes a tablespoon of glue to a cup of shaving cream foam to work. Also provide craft sticks, pencils, several boxes of birthday candles, aprons and a flat place for them to lay while drying. See example of cake.

Children will put their names on the back of their cake and put on their apron. Then they will use the craft sticks to spread onto their cake, the pretend icing (glue, foam, color mixture). Next they will tell how old they are and place that many candles on their cake. Last they will take cake to spot provided to dry.

For a <u>language</u> activity, teacher will have a variety of short picture books. Teacher will encourage children to find a book that they would like to have read to them. When they find a book they like, have them bring it to you during free play and read it to them. Before starting to read it show the book and ask if others would like to hear the story too. If they do, have them join you and the other child and read it to the group.

At the end of this day have children come to circle and sing "Special Me" by Dr. Jean. Then have each child come up and tell how old they are and place that many candles in the pretend cake*. Now teacher will say something nice about that child before each one of them goes home.

*The pretend cake is made by cutting 2 thin layers of Styrofoam into circle shapes the size of a saucer. Then glue them on top of each other and then to the saucer. Now mix food coloring with glue to create the icing. Spread it over the top layer and then place additional glue so that it will drip over the edge. Now place plastic candle holders in the top of the cake. I use five, but if your children are older you can place more. If children are different ages, put largest number of holders for their age and just put less candles in holder. See the example.

Where To Get What You Need

There are many different places to get what you need. If you use your imagination, many items can be substituted for what you have on hand, can get for free, etc. For example, you may have an abundance of baby food jars from a family toddler. You can easily convert these to be part of a project. Teaching is also about being resourceful. Have family, friends, students and yourself save:

- Baby food jars

- Toilet paper rolls

- Paper towel rolls

- Scraps of material

- Extra tile

- Extra pieces from home improvement projects

- Coffee cans

- Oatmeal containers

- 2 liter bottles

- Cereal boxes

- Egg carton

- Milk jugs

- Salt containers

- Anything you can think of to be re-purposed for a learning tool

Other places to get materials include:

- Home improvement stores (Lowes or Home Depot)

- Dollar Stores

- Educational Supply Stores

- Grocery Store

- Party Supply Store

- Online Resources:

  — Oriental Trading Company: www.orientaltrading.com

  — http://www.etacuisenaire.com

  — Many great songs and activities are available from http://www.newbridgeonline.com/, which is where you can find the MacMillan Sing and Learn songs and other activities. Use the search function and type in "songs for learning". You may also be able to find these used online at www.alibris.com, www.amazon.com, or www.abebooks.com.

www.ingramcontent.com/pod-product-compliance
Lightning Source LLC
LaVergne TN
LVHW081319060426
835509LV00015B/1585